AnOther
E. E. Cummings

Selected and introduced by
Richard Kostelanetz
With
John Rocco, Assistant Editor

LIVERIGHT
New York

First published as a Liveright paperback 1999

For information about permission to reproduce selections from this book, write
to Permissions, Liveright Publishing Corporation, 500 Fifth Avenue, New York,
NY 10110.

Manufacturing by The Maple-Vail Book Manufacturing Group.

Library of Congress Cataloging-in-Publication Data
Cummings, E. E. (Edward Estlin), 1894–1962.
    Another E. E. Cummings / selected and introduced by Richard
Kostelanetz ; assistant editor, John Rocco.
        p.   cm.
    Includes index.
    ISBN 0-87140-157-6
    I. Kostelanetz, Richard.   II. Rocco, John (John M.)   III. Title.
PS3505.U334A6   1998
811'.53—DC20   95-45471
                                                                          CIP

ISBN 0-87140-174-6 pbk.

W. W. Norton & Company, Inc.
500 Fifth Avenue, New York, N.Y. 10110
www.wwnorton.com

W. W. Norton & Company Ltd.
Castle House, 75/76 Wells Street, London W1T 3QT

    6 7 8 9 0

ACKNOWLEDGMENTS

For permission to reprint the following material, I am grateful to:

David Diamond and Peer-Southern Organization, Concert Music Division (810 Seventh Ave, New York, NY 10019), for the opening page of David Diamond's "I Shall Imagine Life." Copyright © 1968 by Southern Music Publishing Co., Inc. International Copyright secured. All rights reserved.

C. F. Peters, Inc. (373 Park Avenue South, New York, NY 10016), for the opening pages of scores by John Cage and Morton Feldman, with copyrights attached.

Peter Dickinson (Dept. of Music, Goldsmith College, New Cross, London SE14 6NW, England), for the opening page of *An E. E. Cummings Song Cycle.*

Tetra/Continuo Music Group, Inc. (c/o Bregman, 960 Park Avenue, New York, NY 10028-0325), for the opening page of Peter Schickele's "dim" and "l (a."

Jerome L. Grossman, for his father's French translation of Cummings' "r-p-o-p-h-e-s-s-a-g-r", from *58 + 58 Poem* (Paris 1979).

Mary de Rachewiltz for her Italian translation, from *Poesie* (Einaudi, 1987).

Augusto de Campos, for his Portuguese translation, from *40 poem(a)s of e. e. cummings* (Second ed. Brasiliense, Sao Paulo, Brazil, 1986).

Langewiesche-Brandt KG, D-82067 Ebenhausen (Isartal), for Eva Hesse's German translation. Copyright © Langewiesche-Brandt, Ebenhausen bei Munchen.

Stanisław Baranczak (Cambridge MA), for his Polish translation, from *150 Wierszy* (Wydawnictwo Literackie Kraków, 1994); copyright © 1994 by author and publisher.

Gerald Janecek, for Vladimir Britanishsky's Russian translation, from *Voum!* (Kaluga), No. 2 (3), 1992.

The Dutch translation has been, according to its sometime publisher, "for many years out of print."

Harvard University Press, for "i & you & is" from *i; six nonlectures* by e. e. cummings (The Charles Eliot Norton Lectures 1952–1953). Copyright © 1953 by E. E. Cummings. Copyright © renewed 1981 by E. E. Cummings Trust.

Richard S. Kennedy for the book's epigraph, from *Dreams in the Mirror: A Biography of E. E. Cummings* (Liveright, 1980).

I think [E. E. Cummings] will remain popular for a long time, for several reasons. He is one of the most individual poets who ever lived—and, though it sometimes seems so, it is not just his vices and exaggerations, the defects of his qualities, that make a writer popular. But, primarily, Mr. Cummings' poems are loved because they are full of sentimentality, of sex, of more or less improper jokes, of elementary lyric insistence.

—Randall Jarrell, "The Profession of Poetry" (1950–1)

There is, typically, an intimate connection between the poem's appearance and the proper control of reading rate, emotional evocation, and aesthetic inflection. Indeed, one has the sense, reading these "picture poems" (his phrase) aloud, that one is translating inadequately from one language to another, with proportionate loss to the mere listener. This is an especially striking realization when one remembers that Cummings himself read his poems memorably, indeed read his own work better than any other living poet.

— John Logan, "The Organ-Grinder and the Cockatoo" (1970)

[Guillaume Apollinaire] achieved the final dismemberment of poetry as an exposition in the "calligrammatic" style, often undeniably effective, sometimes merely cute. The visual aptness of these poems is seldom matched by appropriate qualities of sound, which Apollinaire could easily have produced. His idiogrammatic ideas did not find such disciplined application as we find later in E. E. Cummings, Ezra Pound, and Charles Olson.

—Roger Shattuck, *The Banquet Years* (1958)

Taking advantage of the code of the typewriter, with its regular spacing and its vertical and horizontal movements, the American poet E. E. Cummings imploded the configuration of words and reinvented the poetic space with the resulting fragments. His most innovative texts, written in the '20s and onwards, have rigorous structures, often creating visual rhythms with left and right margins, punctuation marks and the alternation between standard upper and lower cases. —Eduardo Kac, "Recent Experiments in Holopoetry and Computer Holopoetry" (1991)

Cummings . . . who has been driven abroad for his two major subjects *(The Enormous Room* and the Russia of *Eimi)* is indelibly New England. And, though it be almost oxymoron to say so, "Whitman's one living descendant."

—Ezra Pound, "National Culture" (1938)

Cummings was . . . the very model of a modern anarchist general; the kinky sexuality—surrogate whores, doll-women, weird dildos, and assorted promiscuities; a ruthless, often funny, self-scrutiny—Cummings looks into a mirror and sees a "clown's smirk in the skull of a baboon" and a "shape who merely eats and turds . . . ere with the dirt death shall him vastly gird"; and the consciously tacky endrhymes, rendered in a music-hall manner. Cummings, never officious, eschewed the pompous and the sententious for a humorous and healthy perspective on himself. If, as he believed, we live in *lower-case times,* there is no need for a self-aggrandizement symbolized by the capital I.

—Robert Peters, *Where the Bee Sucks* (1994)

In contrast to these ambitious arts of progress and development, the paintings, poems, and compositions of the Banquet Years turn back upon themselves and lie quiet. They imply that by being sufficiently still, by becoming for an instant exactly identical with ourselves, nothing more nor less, we can allow the universe to move around us. This is the meaning in art of relativity. An object in motion has difficulty taking into account other motions. Only by achieving rest, *arrest,* can we perceive what is happening outside ourselves. Simultanism, the third voice of life, signifies an approach to immobility and thus an extremely sensitive attunement to the infinite universe. Baudelaire, Bergson, and Cummings are all describing this state.

—Roger Shattuck, *The Banquet Years* (1958)

To the memory of
S. Foster Damon (1893–1971)

S. Foster Damon, a handsome, blond-haired enthusiast of the arts from Newton [MA], who was two years older than Cummings, became his guide to all that was modern in the arts. Damon seemed interested in everything. He was a musician, president of the Harvard Music Society, and editor of the Harvard Music Review, *which was a first-rate periodical, a real testimony to the good taste, maturity, and curiosity of the Harvard aesthetes. He taught Cummings to play the piano (Estlin could already play ragtime by ear) and to write music. He introduced him to Debussy, to Stravinsky, and to the delightful satiric piano sketches of Erik Satie. He took him to the El Greco exhibit at the Fogg Museum, for he considered El Greco "modern." He made him acquainted with the French impressionists, with Cézanne, and with Les Fauves, all of whom had a decided impact on Cummings' later poetry. He took him to the Armory Show in 1913 when it traveled to Boston, and Cummings was ecstatic over the sculptures of Brancusi. He took him to New York after a Harvard-Yale boat race and Cummings was overwhelmed by the "modern Babylon," a different kind of visit from the one he had made years before with his father. Damon was an editor of the* Monthly *[the better of two campus literary magazines], he wrote poetry, he wrote an article on the history of free verse and received a letter from Amy Lowell about it. He took an interest in Wilde, Shaw, Maeterlinck, Whistler, Pirandello. He subscribed to* Poetry *magazine and read Sandburg, Masters, and Lindsay. He owned a rare copy of Gertrude Stein's* Tender Buttons, *which delighted and bewildered Cummings. He owned a copy of Pound's anthology* Des Imagistes *(H.D., Aldington, Flint, Joyce, Hueffer) and by this means brought the Imagist Movement into Cummings' ken. He organized the Harvard Poetry Society in 1915. Besides providing all this cultural excitement, he opened the way to some old-fashioned college activities too: he took Cummings out drinking for the first time in his life. —Richard S. Kennedy,* Dreams in the Mirror *(1980)*

CONTENTS

Preface xiii

Introduction xv

Deviant Traditional Verse 1

Erotic Poetry 43

Language Experiments 75

Visual Poetry and Sound Poetry 139

Texts Set to Music 167

Condensed Prose 185

Elliptical Narratives 205

A Book without a Title 215

Film Scenario 221

Translation 229

Arts Criticism 243

Self-Prefaces 265
   To Ezra Pound 267
   Nonlecture Four: I & You & Is 268
   Introduction to *The Enormous Room* 277
   Why Do You Paint? 280
   No Thanks 281

Memoir 283
    To Whom It May Concern 285
    From *The Enormous Room* 287
    From *Eimi* 292
    To S. Foster Damon 303

Index of Poems
by Opening Lines and Titles 307

PREFACE

I first saw E. E. Cummings (1894–1962) at Brown University around 1959, when he came to give one of the many public performances that dominated his activities in the final years of his life. He was introduced by S. Foster Damon, who had been a professor at Brown for over thirty years and was by then officially emeritus. Only eighteen months older, Damon recalled that he and Cummings had first met at Harvard nearly a half-century before, when in a large lecture hall someone whose name began DA was assigned a seat next to someone whose name began CU. In *i: six nonlectures* (1953) is Cummings' appreciation of Damon, "who opened my eyes and ears not merely to Domenico Theotocopuli (aka El Greco) and William Blake, but to all ultra (at that moment) modern music and poetry and painting." Perhaps because Cummings for his declamation favored his familiar lyrics, Damon turned off his hearing aid and soon fell visibly asleep. By the following year, I sought out Damon and learned about an eccentric tradition of American literature and music and, by extension, about sides of Cummings that were less familiar.

My first appreciation of the more experimental Cummings began as a review of Richard Kennedy's biography, reprinted in my first collection of essays on poetry, *The Old Poetries and the New* (University of Michigan, 1981), where Cummings was indicatively placed in the second half of the book ("The New"), while Ezra Pound, Allen Ginsberg, and John Ashbery, for three touchstones, were placed in the first half. From that point onward, I wanted to do an anthology that would gather in one place this Other Cummings, much as an earlier anthology of mine, *The Yale Gertrude Stein* (1980), identified a more experimental and finally more substantial writer than the familiar author of *Three Lives* and *The Autobiography of Alice B. Toklas.* Though the more innovative Cummings is commonly acknowledged, as is the more innovative Stein, Cummings criticism has usually concentrated on his more accessible writings, and most selections from his work have featured the easier pieces. In this anthology, as in most of my others, it has been my aim not to sweep up behind established opinion but to propose alternative taste and to rescue unfamiliar work. *AnOther Cummings* represents the fruit of twenty-five years of thinking and perhaps a decade of selecting; it differs from many other one-writer selections in that the first person to read it, the first to learn about the possibilities of poetic activity, is meant to be me. The book's chapters represent categories that are scarcely exclusive; more than one poem could fit in another place.

Every effort has been made to trace the ownership of all copyrighted material and to make full acknowledgment of its use. If any error or omission has occurred, it will be corrected in all future editions, provided that appropriate notification is submitted in writing to the Publisher. I am grateful to the University of Michigan Press for permission to reprint portions of my earlier essay, to Victor Schmalzer at W. W. Norton-Liveright for commissioning this book, to George J. Firmage for his definitive texts and for letting me select from books edited by him, to George Stade for permission to use the transcriptions and annotations of Cummings' letters done with F. W. Dupee, to colleagues who supplied me with copies of Cummings materials previously unfamiliar to me, to the dedicatee for the initial education, to Chris Wolf for proofreading, and, most important, to John Rocco for his editorial assistance, his prefaces to the most difficult Cummings texts, and general knowledge about avant-garde literature.

New York, New York, 14 May 1996.

INTRODUCTION

Nothing is quite as easy as using words like some-
body else. We all of us do exactly this nearly all the
time—and when we do it we are not poets.
                                    —E. E. Cummings, in a letter

No one would dispute the opinion that E. E. Cummings (1894–
1962) ranks among the prominent modern American poets.
What is surprising, and thus debatable, is that no other major
American poet of his generation remains so neglected and mis-
understood. Richard S. Kennedy's *Dreams in the Mirror* (1980)
was only the second extended biography of Cummings, while
T. S. Eliot, Ezra Pound, and William Carlos Williams, by compari-
son, have all had several volumes devoted to their lives. Similarly,
native criticism of Cummings' poetry has been comparatively
sparse. Recent histories of American literature have similarly
slighted Cummings. While Daniel Hoffman's conservative *Har-
vard Guide to Contemporary American Writing* (1979) scarcely
acknowledges Cummings' presence, the more self-consciously
progressive *Columbia Literary History of the United States* (1988)
mentions him only a few times, usually in relation to others, and
quotes from his work just once.

Even when Cummings is acknowledged, it is usually for his
more conventional lyric poems. Richard Ellmann's highbrow *The
New Oxford Book of American Verse* (1976) is no different from
Nancy Sullivan's more mundane *Treasury of American Poetry*

(1978) in including *only* his lyrics, while he appears not at all in Helen Vendler's *The Harvard Book of Contemporary American Poetry* (1985), even though he ranks among Harvard's more distinguished literary alumni. Cummings' plays are neglected as well, as they are rarely mentioned in histories of American theater; his critical essays, original though they often were, remain hard to find. Only one scholar, Milton A. Cohen, has written a book about another dimension of his creativity—the paintings and drawings, on which he worked most of his daytimes; indeed, they have never been satisfactorily exhibited or completely examined. Nonetheless, now that the reputations of both Eliot and Pound appear to be receding, it is time, after the centenary of Cummings' birth, to reconsider his career and to concentrate upon what makes him different from his contemporaries—his more inventive writings and larger artistic interests.

Unlike his predecessors, Eliot or Williams, Cummings was for all of his life a full-time writer/artist whose life should be valued only for his contributions to the arts he practiced—and not for anything else. His social philosophy was a visceral libertarianism that was more agreeable than profound—invariably relevant to political situations immediately at hand, as he consistently saw and reacted to the world as an individual, but scarcely rich enough to establish a substantial political position. His criticisms of technology and, at times, of urban life were more successfully elaborated by others. His esthetics were largely anti-high cult. In contrast to Eliot and Pound, Cummings fortunately had neither economic ideas nor a philosophy of history. Some of his affectations were disaffecting, such as not capitalizing the first person singular. (Spelling his name entirely in lower-case letters was someone else's invention that should be forgotten.) Perhaps because he devoted most of his days to painting and to drawing—because art was his full-time profession—the main preoccupation of his poetry is with creation, and specifically with the creation, and thus the experience, of unusual English language.

What survives of Cummings and his work are not his ideas, but first, poems that radically enlarge our sense of linguistic possibilities and, second, a career that enlarges our sense of professional poets' possibilities.

As the epigraph to this essay suggests, Cummings observed a clear distinction between ordinary speech and poetry. The former was common language; the latter, exceptional language. Thus, contrary to current fashion, he enthusiastically used such traditional devices as meter, alliteration, resonant line breaks, and even rhyme. As late as 1957, in the wake of America's inaction in the 1956 Hungarian revolution, he produced a poem, "Thanksgiving (1956)," that closed with this biting satirical ditty:

> So rah-rah-rah democracy
> let's all be thankful as hell
> and bury the statue of liberty
> (because it begins to smell)

However, what distinguished Cummings from the other rhyming poets was his sense that traditional devices hardly sufficed; he created new ones which would function to enhance language poetically. He was, from his first book to his last, an incomparably inventive poet.

One of his fundamental motives was breaking apart the traditionally geometric format of poetry. Instead of always using rectangular blocks of type with flush-left margins, Cummings often placed his poems on the page in a rich variety of alternative shapes like these, among others:

The point of these experiments was not just creating attractive designs but sensitively varying the reader's perception of printed language. More than any of his major contemporaries, he knew what could be gained by enlarging or reducing or even eliminating the horizontal spacing between consecutive words. He saw that the vertically rectangular page of the book was itself a poetic field that could be filled variously and that a distinctive image on the page could in itself enhance a poem. It was amazing how many designs he could make that are, even now, uniquely identifiable as his.

A second rich Cummings device was the use of one part of speech to function in place of another. Thus, verbs sometimes appear as nouns:

> my father moved through dooms of love
> through sames of am through haves of give

As Malcolm Cowley carefully observed in the *New Republic* (Jan. 27, 1932), nouns also "become verbs ('but if a look should april me') or they become adverbs by adding 'ly,' or superlative adjectives by adding 'est' (thus, instead of writing 'most like a girl,' Cummings has 'girlest'). Adjectives, adverbs, and conjunctions, too, become participles by adding 'ing' ('onlying,' 'softlying,' 'whying'); participles become adverbs by adding 'ly' ('kneelingly')."

Phonetic spellings could be poetically used not only for wit, as in "the hoe tell days are teased" for a classy Manhattan residence known as the Hotel des Artistes or "Gay-Pay-Oo" for the Soviet secret police (G.P.U.). Phonetic spellings also represent spoken dialect:

> oil tel duh woil doi sez
> dooyuh unners tanmih eesez pullih nizmus tash, oi

On more accessible levels, Cummings doubled words for emphasis, much as Malayans do—"slowlyslow." He used prefixes such as "un," "im," or "not" and then suffixes such as "ing" and "ingly" to modify their root word in various subtle ways. A favorite epithet, "unalive," is not synonymous with dead.

He recognized that individual words could be expressively taken apart:

```
                    r-p-o-p-h-e-s-s-a-g-r
              who
        a)s w(e loo)k
        upnowgath
                PPEGORHRASS
                        eringint(o-
        aThe):1
            eA
              !p:
    S                                       a
                    (r
        rIvInG                  .gRrEaPsPhOs)
                                    to
        rea(be)rran(com)gi(e)ngly
        ,grasshopper;
```

rendering not only a distinct visual image (especially on a vertically rectangular page) but visually enhancing the connotations of the key word. As Harvey Gross noted in *Sound and Form in Modern Poetry* (1969), "Actually, the poem does not so much *look like* the grasshopper's action as give the feel of action. Cummings uses an elaborate technique of synaesthesia, a complex visual and aural derangement to signify emotional meaning."

Here he is less a painter than a choreographer portraying movement in design and incidentally reflecting the temporal revolution implicit in Marcel Duchamp's *Nude Descending a Staircase* (1911). Incidentally, Cummings may have been the first American writer to discover a truth initially familiar to modernist architects—that less could be more.

He who had taken words apart could also combine them ingeniously, telescoping language and gaining resonance by omitting spaces—creating in English a reasonable ersatz German with such conjunctions as "bookofpoems," "curselaughgroping," "driftwhirlfully," "thankyouverymuch," and "truebeautifly." Cummings found expressive possibilities even in punctuation marks, as no one before or since has used hyphens and semicolons so resonantly. The single word 'taps" is considerably different when punctuated, as Cummings did, "t,a,p,s." In the middle of a poem about acrobats, he writes:

> hes shes
> &meet&
> swoop

with the ampersands adding effects that would otherwise be lost. In a comparative sense, some of his discoveries are incredibly, perhaps dubiously, simple; but the point is that no poet before him dared use such elementary enhancements. The refusal to give titles to most of his poems represents evasion to some and integrity to me. Compared to his more pretentious contemporaries, Cummings had a casual sense of poetry that remains attractive.

He discovered, too, that properties within typeset language, such as capitalization, could contribute to poetic communication (and that a Greenwich Village neighbor, S. A. Jacobs, could be his loyal typesetter). "SpRiN,k,LiNG" has ideographic connotations that "sprinkling" lacks; "mOOn" is more evocative than "moon." Cummings' recorded declamations of his work demonstrate how unusual typography prompts spoken rhythms that are quite different from those engendered by conventional poetic scoring.

The placement of words in space could also introduce kinetic qualities that would be impossible to achieve in conventional poetic design. The theme of his "grasshopper" poem, quoted earlier, is a certain kind of insect movement. The point of the following passage from number XIII in "Portraits" is a representation of a change in pace:

pho

nographisrunn
ingd o w, n   phonograph
                    stopS.

In the foreword to *Is 5* (1926), one of his few statements on his purposes, Cummings spoke specifically of creating "that precision which creates movement." To put it differently, typography could function like musical notation.

The opening poem in *1 × 1* (1944), which appears here on page 162, presages the current interest in poetic abstraction, its words and phrases cohering in terms not of syntax or semantics but of diction, meter, and other qualities indigenous to poetry. Cummings also wrote pure *sound* poetry, in which acoustic qualities become the principle elements of both coherence and enhancement. In *W[ViVa]* (1931) is a poem, prefaced "from the cognoscenti," which opens:

bingbongwhom chewchoo
laugh dingle nails personally
bung loamhome picpac
obviously scratches tomorrowlobs

and continues in a similar style to a single line which is set below and to the left of the six four-line rectangles: "of radarw leschin," which suggests that only a radical change in language can realize a *revolution*. Though Cummings was nearly an exact contemporary of Vladimir Mayakovsky (1893–1930), the two never met and probably had no effect upon each other; nonetheless, Cummings illustrates Mayakovsky's dictum: "Neologisms are obligatory in writing poetry."

Despite all of his formalist ambitions, Cummings was also a personal poet whose ideas on everything, from sex to politics, were based upon his own experience. As his first major American critic, Norman Friedman, observed back in 1960, the "five major forms" of his poetry are:

> the description, that locates its speaker in the presence of some sensory stimulus and represents him as perceiving; praise and eulogy, that place him in relation to some person, type, or idea, and represent him as admiring; the satire, that places him in relation to society and that represents him as its critic; reflection, that places him before scenes and people and represents him as interpreting and commenting; and persuasion, that places him in the presence of someone else and represents him as speaking to him or her.

In most cases, the first-person voice represents Cummings himself.

At his Harvard commencement in 1915, Cummings delivered a stunningly prophetic lecture on "The New Art" that featured a sensitive appreciation of Gertrude Stein. Perhaps it was from her that he learned about the esthetic advantages of an intentionally limited vocabulary. In his collection *No Thanks* (1938) is the extraordinary poem beginning "brIght" that appears here on page 85. It contains only eleven discrete words, all six letters or less in length. The eleven words are successfully broken apart and nonsyntactically recombined to form fifteen lines of forty-four words—all three-letter words appearing thrice, all four letter words four times, etc. With this rigorous structure and others Cummings presaged several formal innovations that have since become more prominent in contemporary avant-garde poetry. The fact that Cummings discovered these present possibilities several decades ago should contribute to his current stature.

While many of the lyrics remain familiar, what is not so commonly known is his other artistic activities. Cummings wrote plays as well as formally dramatic sketches meant to be read, rather than performed; he was among the first American writers to script a film scenario ("A Pair of Jacks," 1925) and a ballet (*Tom*, 1935). Among his works are innovative masterpieces of experimental prose. He wrote important criticism, not only of poetry but of theater, and was perhaps the first American drama critic to concentrate not upon formal work that was presented in legitimate theaters but upon vaudeville, burlesque, animated films, and even the informal theatricals available at the Coney Island amusement park. He did literary translations that are still used. Even his correspondence is distinctive.

One reason why our understanding of Cummings has been so deficient is that his work has never been fully available. His *Complete Poems 1904–1962* did not appear until 1991, replacing an earlier "complete" edition limited to "1913–1962." His major text of innovative prose, *Eimi* (1933), has been out of print for years, as have his two shorter plays and the ballet *Tom*, as well as George Firmage's *A Miscellany* (1958, 1965), which reprints previously uncollected prose. Only a small percentage of Cummings' visual art has ever been reproduced.

Cummings probably worked as hard at his paintings and drawings as he did at his writing, the former being done by day and the latter at night. More than 2,000 completed paintings exist; the Houghton Library at Harvard reportedly has over 10,000 sheets of drawings. His literary eminence notwithstanding, Cummings had remarkably few exhibitions and scarce dealer representation. It is hard for most of us to know the quality of this visual work, not to mention how it looks. Some early pieces were reproduced in *CIOPW* (1931), a limited $9^1/_2$-by-$12^1/_2$-inch clothbound book whose title is an acronym for the painterly media in which Cummings worked: charcoal, ink, oil, pencil, and watercolor. However, this scarce book has never been reissued. The absence of at least a "Selected Drawings and Paintings" raises questions about Cummings' other art: Was he like Wyndham Lewis—a literary polyartist who excelled at both visual and verbal arts? Or was he a Henry David Thoreau, whose drawings were merely curious? Or should his mix of art and writing be placed somewhere in between? Regardless, his career showed that one could spend a lifetime earnestly practicing more than one art, in spite of gross discrepancies in recognition.

Even though Cummings insisted upon living entirely off his writings, readings, and art (and compromised only once, when he became the Charles Eliot Norton Professor of Poetry for a year at Harvard), he received remarkably few awards and even fewer fellowships. The literary powermen of his time tend to regard him as an inconsequential eccentric—an agreeable lyric poet whose disagreeable "gimmicky" experiments undermined his reputation. They inevitably preferred his aphorisms to his inventions, though aphorisms do not a major poet make. Not unlike Stein (who also studied at Harvard) he had to publish conventional work for his more radical work to be considered seriously. Some pundits could never excuse Cummings from failing to write the kind of pretentious long poem they had come to identify with modern masterhood, for he was to his end a sprinter more comfortable with short poems and small paintings. Though academics could never forgive him for failing to pass through the distinct stages of a poetic career, what was really more extraordinary the more one thinks about it, was how much of his mature poetic style, including his radical renovations of traditional poetic forms (especially the sonnet) and the more experimental directions, was fully present in his very first book. In other words, the more avant-garde Cummings—the kind of work favored here—comes not from a single period of his writings but from every decade of his career. For much of his life, Cummings lacked a regular publisher, and two of his collections were initially self-published. (One, in 1935, was pointedly entitled *No Thanks* and audaciously dedicated to the fourteen publishers who previously refused it!)

Let me suggest the opposite of the conventional view. If you favor the lyric verse ("my father moved . . . ," etc.), while excluding the radical poetry, Cummings is indeed a minor figure. However, there is another, better Cummings—the most inventive American poet of his time, the truest successor to Whitman and in poetry the peer of Charles Ives and Gertrude Stein. If you focus upon Cummings' more extraordinary poems—those that distinguish him from everyone else, before or since—you are more likely to recognize him, as I do, as the major American poet of the middle-twentieth century. If you focus upon his integrities, beginning with his refusal to title most of his poems and the creation of works that were (and still are) so easily identifiable as his (and could thus be feasibly published without his name), and including his fulltime devotion to his arts (in contrast to poets who have been publishers, professors, and doctors), he becomes not only a persuasive professional model but a major American poet.

DEVIANT
TRADITIONAL
VERSE

I have to go on tryin' to tell you. And I now tell you
that your Mr. Cummings is a very great writer, I tell
you he follows H. James, and Thoreau, and Whitman.
I tell you he is the most intelligent man in America.
   —Ezra Pound, "E. E. Cummings Examined" (1942)

When I was at college some thirty-plus years ago, Cummings'
college buddy S. Foster Damon (1893–1971) taught "verse writ-
ing," where we were required to do a series of exercises with
traditional English forms, beginning with Chaucerian stress verse.
My assumption is that this course probably reflected the training
to which Damon and Cummings had subjected themselves as
aspiring poets. One difference was that Cummings, at once a
conservative and a radical, deviated from traditional forms at the
same time that he acknowledged them, beginning with couplets
but producing mostly sonnets. It is scarcely surprising that no
other modern poet produced so many variations on the fourteen-
line poem, continually honoring the form as he was expanding
it—*defamiliarizing* with a wealth of alternatives, including
poems whose broken lines (representing the literary equivalent
of musical rests) must be counted carefully for the reader to

ascertain that there are indeed fourteen. A further deviation was that many of Cummings' sonnets have distinctly modern erotic content. This section opens with couplets and includes his renovation of the traditional political ballad.

1

guilt is the cause of more disauders
than history's most obscene marorders

2

mr youse needn't be so spry
concernin questions arty

each has his tastes but as for i
i likes a certain party

gimme the he-man's solid bliss
for youse ideas i'll match youse

a pretty girl who naked is
is worth a million statues

3

serene immediate silliest and whose
vast one function being to enter a Toy and
emerging(believably enlarged)make how
many stopped millions of female hard for their
millions of stopped male to look at(now
-fed infantile eyes drooling unmind
grim yessing childflesh perpetually acruise
and her quick way of slowly staring and such hair)
the Californian handpicked thrill mechanically
packed and released for all this very diminishing
vicarious ughhuh world(the pertly papped
muchmouthed)her way of beginningly finishing
(and such hair)the expensively democratic tyrannically
dumb

Awake,chaos:we have napped.

4

           she,straddling my lap,
hinges(wherewith I tongue each eager pap)
and,reaching down,by merely fingertips
the hungry Visitor steers to love's lips
Whom(justly as she now begins to sit,
almost by almost giving her sweet weight)
O,how those hot thighs juicily embrace!
and (instant by deep instant)as her face
watches,scarcely alive,that magic Feast
greedily disappearing least by least—
through what a dizzily palpitating host
(sharp inch by inch)swoons sternly my huge Guest!
until(quite when our touching bellies dream)
unvisibly love's furthest secrets rhyme.

5

I have seen her a stealthily frail
flower walking with its fellows in the death
of light,against whose enormous curve of flesh
exactly cubes of tiny fragrance try;
i have watched certain petals rapidly wish
in the corners of her youth;whom,fiercely shy
and gently brutal,the prettiest wrath
of blossoms dishevelling made a pale
fracas upon the accurate moon....
Across the important gardens her body
will come toward me with its hurting sexual smell
of lilies....beyond night's silken immense swoon
the moon is like a floating silver hell
a song of adolescent ivory.

6

i like my body when it is with your
body.   It is so quite new a thing.
Muscles better and nerves more.
i like your body.   i like what it does,
i like its hows.   i like to feel the spine
of your body and its bones,and the trembling
-firm-smooth ness and which i will
again and again and again
kiss,   i like kissing this and that of you,
i like,slowly stroking the,shocking fuzz
of your electric fur,and what-is-it comes
over parting flesh....And eyes big love-crumbs,

and possibly i like the thrill

of under me you so quite new

7

in making Marjorie god hurried
a boy's body on unsuspicious
legs of girl. his left hand quarried
the quartzlike face. his right slapped
the amusing big vital vicious
vegetable of her mouth.
Upon the whole he suddenly clapped
a tiny sunset of vermouth
-colour.   Hair. he put between
her lips a moist mistake,whose fragrance hurls
me into tears,as the dusty new-
ness of her obsolete gaze begins to.   lean....
a little against me,when for two
dollars i fill her hips with boys and girls

8

if a cheerfulest Elephantangelchild should sit

(holding a red candle over his head
by a finger of trunk,and singing out of a red

book)on a proud round cloud in a white high night

where his heartlike ears have flown adorable him
self tail and all(and his tail's red christmas bow)
—and if,when we meet again,little he(having flown
even higher)is sunning his penguinsoul in the glow

of a joy which wasn't and isn't and won't be words

while possibly not(at a guess)quite half way down
to the earth are leapandswooping tinily birds
whose magical gaiety makes your beautiful name—

i feel that(false and true are merely to know)
Love only has ever been,is,and will ever be,So

helves surling out of eakspeasies per(reel)hapsingly
proregress heandshe-ingly people
trickle curselaughgroping shrieks bubble
squirmwrithed staggerful unstrolls collaps ingly
flash a of-faceness stuck thumblike into pie
is traffic this recalls hat gestures bud
plumptumbling hand voices Eye Doangivuh sud-
denly immense impotently Eye Doancare Eye
And How replies the upsquirtingly careens
the to collide flatfooting with Wushyuhname
a girl-flops to the Geddup curb leans
carefully spewing into her own Shush Shame

as(out from behind Nowhere)creeps the deep thing
everybody sometimes calls morning

10

that which we who're alive in spite of mirrors
(have died beyond the clock)we,of ourselves

who more a part are(less who are aware)

than of my books could even be your shelves
(that which we die for;not when or unless
if or to prove,imperfectly or since

but through spontaneous deft strictly horrors

which stars may not observe;while roses wince)
that which we die for lives(may never cease
views with smooth vigilant perpetual eyes
each exact victim,how he does not stir)

O love,my love!soul clings and heart conceives

and mind leaps(and that which we die for lives
as wholly as that which we live for dies)

11

She smiled. She was too full of Bud and siph
to be pretty,even at a distance. These made her
only beautiful....Now,as she laid her
five fingers on the unwhite stiff
cloth,I breathed. With her sat a stiff
I'd seen before somewhere or other. Her pimp
was watching from the bar—her eyes went limp
and big,so blaming big it was a if ...
and hungry.... "So,he says to me Girlie
he says,you're all in from them rye-highs.
Cut it. I give him a glawnce,and I says,Jawn
I says ..." My spine scuttled,fed by pale curly
memories;I started half to rise,
and the curtain of the booth was drawn.

This marvelous Petrarchan sonnet was uncovered by Richard S. Kennedy among Cummings' unpublished manuscripts. The classical form frames an ugly scene and fragments of dialogue.

structure,miraculous challenge,devout am

upward deep most invincible unthing
—stern sexual timelessness,outtowering
this noisy impotence of not and same

answer,beginning,ecstasy,to dare:
prouder than all mountains,more than all
oceans various
                            and while everywhere
beneath thee and about thyself a small
hoping insect,humanity,achieves
(moult beyond difficult moult)amazing doom
who standest as thou hast stood and thou shalt stand.

Nor any dusk but kneelingly believes
thy secret and each morning stoops to blend

her star with what huge merciful forms presume

13

you asked me to come:it was raining a little,
and the spring;a clumsy brightness of air
wonderfully stumbled above the square,
little amorous-tadpole people wiggled

battered by stuttering pearl,
                              leaves jiggled
to the jigging fragrance of newness
—and then.   My crazy fingers liked your dress
....your kiss,your kiss was a distinct brittle

flower,and the flesh crisp set
my love-tooth on edge.   So until light
each having each we promised to forget—

wherefore is there nothing left to guess:
the cheap intelligent thighs,the electric trite
thighs;the hair stupidly priceless.

14

O Thou to whom the musical white spring

offers her lily inextinguishable,
taught by thy tremulous grace bravely to fling

Implacable death's mysteriously sable
robe from her redolent shoulders,
                                    Thou from whose
feet reincarnate song suddenly leaping
flameflung,mounts,inimitably to lose
herself where the wet stars softly are keeping

their exquisite dreams—O Love! upon thy dim
shrine of intangible commemoration,
(from whose faint close as some grave languorous hymn

pledged to illimitable dissipation
unhurried clouds of incense fleetly roll)

i spill my bright incalculable soul.

when you went away it was morning
(that is,big horses;light feeling up
streets;heels taking derbies (where?) a pup
hurriedly hunched over swill;one butting

trolley imposingly empty;snickering
shop doors unlocked by white-grub
faces) clothes in delicate hubbub

as you stood thinking of anything,

maybe the world....But i have wondered since
isn't it odd of you really to lie
a sharp agreeable flower between my

amused legs
    kissing with little dints

of april,making the obscene shy
breasts tickle,laughing when i wilt and wince

utterly and amusingly i am pash
possibly because
                    .dusk and if it
perhaps drea-mingly Is(not-
quite trees hugging with the rash,
coherent light
)only to trace with
stiffening slow shrill eyes beyond a fit-
and-cling of stuffs the alert willing myth
of body,which will make oddly to strut
my indolent priceless smile,
                                        until
this very frail enormous star(do you see
it?)and this shall dance upon the nude
and final silence and shall the
(i do but touch you)timid lewd
moon plunge skilfully into the hill.

17

my deathly body's deadly lady

smoothly-foolish exquisitely,tooled
(becoming exactly passionate Gladly

grips with chuckles of supreme sex

my mute-articulate protrusion)
Inviting my gorgeous bullet to vex

the fooling groove intuitive...

And the sharp ripples-of-her-brain bite
fondly into mine,
                as the slow give-

of-hot-flesh Takes,me;in crazier waves of light
sweetsmelling
                fragrant:
                        unspeakable chips
Hacked,
        from the immense sun(whose day is drooled
on night—)and the abrupt ship-of-her lips

disintegrates,with a coy!explosion

18

oil tel duh woil doi sez
dooyuh unnurs tanmih eesez pullih nizmus tash,oi
dough un giv uh shid oi sez.   Tom
oidoughwuntuh doot,butoiguttuh
braikyooz,datswut eesez tuhmih.   (Nowoi askyuh
woodundat maik yurarstoin
green?   Oilsaisough.)—Hool
spairruh luckih?   Thangzkeed.   Mairsee.
Muh jax awl gawn.   Fur Croi saik
ainnoughbudih gutnutntuhplai?

HAI

yoozwidduhpoimnuntwaiv un duhyookuhsumpnruddur
givusuhtoonunduhphugnting

american critic ad 1935

alias faggoty slob with a sob in whose cot
tony onceaweek whisper winsomely pul

ling their wool over 120 mil
lion goats each and every one a spot
less lamb
            :nothing in any way sugge

stive
      ;nothing to which anyone might possibly obje

ct
    .& you know all he's got to do is just men
tion something & it sells ten 000 copies.won

derful.isn't it that poor man must read all the time.

read why i'd read in my sleep for half that mon
ey.you don't mean he.did i say anything again

st.wasn't that a.wasn't it.by what was the.such a funny name)

into which world is noone born alive

20

Space being(don't forget to remember)Curved
(and that reminds me who said o yes Frost
Something there is which isn't fond of walls)

an electromagnetic(now I've lost
the)Einstein expanded Newton's law preserved
conTinuum(but we read that beFore)

of Course life being just a Reflex you
know since Everything is Relative or

to sum it All Up god being Dead(not to

mention inTerred)
                    LONG LIVE that Upwardlooking
Serene Illustrious and Beatific
Lord of Creation,MAN:
                    at a least crooking
of Whose compassionate digit,earth's most terrific

quadruped swoons into billiardBalls!

21

her careful distinct sex whose sharp lips comb

my mumbling gropeofstrength(staggered by the lug
of love)
        sincerely greets,with an occult shrug
asking Through her Muteness will slowly roam
my dumbNess?

              her other,wet,warm

lips limp,across my bruising smile;
as rapidly upon the jiggled norm

of agony my grunting eyes pin tailored flames
Her being at this instant commits

an impenetrable transparency.
the harsh erecting breasts and uttering tits
punish my hug
              presto!

                  the bright rile
of jovial hair extremely frames

the face in a hoop of grim ecstasy

the comedian stands on a corner,the sky is
ve   ry   soF.   t Ly. Fal,   Ling   (snow

with a limousines the and whisk of swiftly taxis God

knows howmany mouths eyes bodies
fleetly going into nothing,

verysky the and.of all is,slow-
Ly.faLLing
        ,f all in g)FaLlInG   odd
....which will. swiftly Hug   kiss   or

a drunken Man bangs silentl Y   into the moo
                                n
the comedian is standing.   On a corner   in-a-dream
of.(sn)ow,
          in the nib; bling tune
OF
    "nextwehave the famous dancing team
swiftness & nothing
                  ,letergo
                      Professor!

23

when
        from a sidewalk
                out of(blown never quite to
-gether by large sorry)creatures out
of(clumsily shining out of)instru-
ments,waltzing;undigestibly:groans.bounce

!o-ras-ourh an-dorg-an ble-at-ssw-ee-t-noth ings orarancidhurd
ygurdygur glingth umpssomet hings(whi,le sp,arrow,s wince
among those skeletons of these trees)
                                when
                                        sunbeams loot
furnished rooms through whose foul windows absurd
clouds cruise nobly ridiculous skies

(the;mselve;s a;nd scr;a;tch-ing lousy full.of.rain
beggars yaw:nstretchy:awn)
                        then,
                                o my love
                                        ,then
it's Spring
        immortal Always & lewd shy New

and upon the beyond imagining spasm rise
we
    you-with-me
                around(me)you
                        IYou

24

emptied.hills.listen.
,not,alive,trees,dream(
ev:ery:wheres:ex:tend:ing:hush

)
 andDark
IshbusY
ing-roundly-dis

tinct;chuck
lings,laced
ar:e.by(

fleet&panelike&frailties
!throughwhich!brittlest!whitewhom!
f
  l o a t ?)
            r
        h y t h m s

25

that famous fatheads find that each
   and every thing must have an end
(the silly cause of trivial which
   thinkless unwishing doth depend

   upon the texture of their p-ss)
isn't(and that it mayn't be twirled
   around your little finger is)
what's right about the g. o. world

what's wrong with(between me and we)
   the g -- d -ld w. isn't that it
can't exist(and is that the
   g. o. w. is full of)delete

26

kumrads die because they're told)
kumrads die before they're old
(kumrads aren't afraid to die
kumrads don't
and kumrads won't
believe in life)and death knows whie

(all good kumrads you can tell
by their altruistic smell
moscow pipes good kumrads dance)
kumrads enjoy
s.freud knows whoy
the hope that you may mess your pance

every kumrad is a bit
of quite unmitigated hate
(travelling in a futile groove
god knows why)
and so do i
(because they are afraid to love

27

the boys i mean are not refined
they go with girls who buck and bite
they do not give a fuck for luck
they hump them thirteen times a night

one hangs a hat upon her tit
one carves a cross in her behind
they do not give a shit for wit
the boys i mean are not refined

they come with girls who bite and buck
who cannot read and cannot write
who laugh like they would fall apart
and masturbate with dynamite

the boys i mean are not refined
they cannot chat of that and this
they do not give a fart for art
they kill like you would take a piss

they speak whatever's on their mind
they do whatever's in their pants
the boys i mean are not refined
they shake the mountains when they dance

BALLAD OF AN INTELLECTUAL

Listen,you morons great and small
to the tale of an intellectuall
(and if you don't profit by his career
don't ever say Hoover gave nobody beer).

'Tis frequently stated out where he was born
that a rose is as weak as its shortest thorn:
they spit like quarters and sleep in their boots
and anyone dies when somebody shoots
and the sheriff arrives after everyone's went;
which isn't,perhaps,an environment
where you would(and I should)expect to find
overwhelming devotion to things of the mind.
But when it rains chickens we'll all catch larks
—to borrow a phrase from Karl the Marks.

As a child he was puny;shrank from noise
hated the girls and mistrusted the boise,
didn't like whisky,learned to spell
and generally seemed to be going to hell;
so his parents,encouraged by desperation,
gave him a classical education
(and went to sleep in their boots again
out in the land where women are main).

You know the rest:a critic of note,
a serious thinker,a lyrical pote,
lectured on Art from west to east
—did sass-seyeity fall for it? Cheast!
if a dowager balked at our hero's verse
he'd knock her cold with a page from Jerse;
why,he used to say to his friends,he used
"for getting a debutante give me Prused"
and many's the heiress who's up and swooned
after one canto by Ezra Pooned
(or—to borrow a cadence from Karl the Marx—
a biting chipmunk never barx).

But every bathtub will have its gin
and one man's sister's another man's sin
and a hand in the bush is a stitch in time
and Aint It All A Bloody Shime
and he suffered a fate which is worse than death
and I don't allude to unpleasant breath.

Our blooming hero awoke,one day,
to find he had nothing whatever to say:
which I might interpret(just for fun)
as meaning the es of a be was dun
and I mightn't think(and you mightn't,too)
that a Five Year Plan's worth a Gay Pay Oo
and both of us might irretrievably pause
ere believing that Stalin is Santa Clause:
which happily proves that neither of us
is really an intellectual cus.

For what did our intellectual do,
when he found himself so empty and blo?
he pondered a while and he said,said he
"It's the social system,it isn't me!
Not I am a fake,but America's phoney!
Not I am no artist,but Art's bologney!
Or—briefly to paraphrase Karl the Marx—
'The first law of nature is,trees will be parx.'"

Now all you morons of sundry classes
(who read the Times and who buy the Masses)
if you don't profit by his career
don't ever say Hoover gave nobody beer.

For whoso conniveth at Lenin his dream
shall dine upon bayonets,isn't and seam
and a miss is as good as a mile is best
for if you're not bourgeois you're Eddie Gest
and wastelands live and waistlines die,
which I very much hope it won't happen to eye;
or as comrade Shakespeare remarked of old
All that Glisters Is Mike Gold

(but a rolling snowball gathers no sparks
—and the same hold true of Karl the Marks).

29

EARLY SUMMER SKETCH

The rain
Drips down
O'er fields
All green
With grain.

Earth's gown
Is seen
Clinging
To her
In folds
Bedraggled.

The grey
Sky yields
Great drops
Down-winging
O'er tops
Of fir
And wolds
Green-gay
With Summer,
The new-comer.

For sod
Has haggled
With sky.

The tears
Fall fast
On high.

Aghast
And Dazed
Earth stands,
And lifts
Her hands,
To see
The wrong
Which she
Has done.

The sun
Breaks out
And sears
The drifts
Of cloud
That float
Along.

The shroud
No longer
Low-lies.

The note
Of the song
Of the bird
Is heard.

The cloud
Is furled.

Earth cries
A shout
Of gladness.

O'er skies,
And trees,
And leaf,
And leas
Of bay
Breaks day.

30

of evident invisibles
exquisite the hovering

at the dark portals

of hurt girl eyes

sincere with wonder

a poise a wounding
a beautiful suppression

the accurate boy mouth

now droops the faun head

now the intimate flower dreams

of parted lips
dim upon the syrinx

whereas by dark really released,the modern
flame of her indomitable body
uses a careful fierceness.   Her lips study
my head gripping for a decision:burn
the terrific fingers which grapple and joke
on my passionate anatomy
oh yes!   Large legs pinch,toes choke—
hair-thin strands of magic agony
....by day this lady in her limousine

oozes in fashionable traffic,just
a halfsmile (for society's sweet sake)
in the not too frail lips almost discussed;
between her and ourselves a nearly-opaque
perfume disinterestedly obscene.

32

god gloats upon Her stunning flesh.   Upon
the reachings of Her green body among
unseen things,things obscene (Whose fingers young

the caving ages curiously con)

—but the lunge of Her hunger softly flung
over the gasping shores
                              leaves his smile wan,
and his blood stopped hears in the frail anon

the shovings and the lovings of Her tongue.

god Is The Sea.   All terrors of his being
quake before this its hideous Work most old
Whose battening gesture prophecies a freeing

of ghostly chaos
                       in this dangerous night
through moaned space god worships God—

                                        (behold!
where chaste stars writhe captured in brightening fright)

33

light cursed falling in a singular block
her,rain-warm-naked
     exquisitely hashed

(little careful hunks-of-lilac laughter splashed
from the world prettily upward,mock
us....)
   and there was a clock. tac-tic. tac-toc.

Time and lilacs....minutes and love....do you?and
always
   (i simply understand
the gnashing petals of sex which lock
me seriously.

     Dumb for a while.my

god—a patter of kisses,the chewed stump

of a mouth,huge dropping of a flesh from
hinging thighs
     ....merci....i want to die
nous sommes heureux

      My soul a limp lump

of lymph
   she kissed
    and i

      ....chéri....nous sommes

34

the bed is not very big

a sufficient pillow shoveling
her small manure-shaped head

one sheet on which distinctly wags

at times the weary twig
of a neckless nudity
(very occasionally budding

a flabby algebraic odour

jigs
    et tout en face
always wiggles the perfectly dead
finger of thitherhithering gas.

clothed with a luminous fur

poilu

    a Jesus sags
in frolicsome wooden agony).

35

the poem her belly marched through me as
one army.   From her nostrils to her feet

she smelled of silence.   The inspired cleat

of her glad leg pulled into a sole mass
my separate lusts
                    her hair was like a gas
evil to feel.   Unwieldy....

                            the bloodbeat
in her fierce laziness tried to repeat
a trick of syncopation Europe has

—. One day i felt a mountain touch me where
i stood (maybe nine miles off).   It was spring

sun-stirring.   sweetly to the mangling air
muchness of buds mattered.   a valley spilled
its tickling river in my eyes,
                            the killed

world wriggled like a twitched string.

36

F is for foetus(a

punkslapping
mobsucking
gravypissing poppa but
who just couldn't help it no

matter how hard he never tried)the

great pink
superme
diocri
ty of

a hyperhypocritical D

mocra
c(sing
down with the fascist beast
boom

boom)two eyes

for an eye four
teeth for a tooth
(and the wholly babble open at
blessed are the peacemuckers)

$ $ $ etc(as

the boodle's bent is the
crowd inclined it's
freedom from freedom
the common man wants)

honey swoRkey mollypants

mortals)

climbi
     ng i
     nto eachness begi
     n
dizzily
       swingthings
of speeds of
trapeze gush somersaults
open ing
       hes shes
&meet&
      swoop
         fully is are ex
              quisite theys of re
turn
    a
    n
    d
fall which now drop who all dreamlike

(im

EROTIC POETRY

Cummings is the living presence of the drive to make all our convictions evident by penetrating through their costumes to the living flesh of the matter. He avoids the cliche first by avoiding the whole accepted modus of english. He does it, not to be "popular," God knows, nor to sell anything, but to lay bare the actual experience of love, let us say, in the chance terms which his environment happens to make apparent to him.

—*William Carlos Williams,*
"Lower Case Cummings" (1946)

What is commonly known, but rarely acknowledged in critical print, is that Cummings was the finest erotic poet of his generation. Adventurous in his choice of forms, Cummings was also audacious in his choice of subjects. Where his predecessors wrote of "love," he portrayed copulation not once but many times—variously, wittily and lusciously. His only rivals in American poetry for inventive sexual metaphors appear in that collective literature called "the blues" (where, for instance, Blind Lemon Jefferson made "crocheting" his euphemism for cunnilingus). It is fair to say that E. E. Cummings did for American poetry what Henry Miller did for American prose; for obvious reasons, beginning with blatancy, the latter got a lot more credit.

1

out of bigg

est the knownun
barn
's
on tiptoe darkne

ss

boyandgirl
come
into a s
unwor

ld 2 to

be blessed by
floating
are
shadows of ove

r us-you-me a

n
g
e
l

s

2

may i feel said he
(i'll squeal said she
just once said he)
it's fun said she

(may i touch said he
how much said she
a lot said he)
why not said she

(let's go said he
not too far said she
what's too far said he
where you are said she)

may i stay said he
(which way said she
like this said he
if you kiss said she

may i move said he
is it love said she)
if you're willing said he
(but you're killing said she

but it's life said he
but your wife said she
now said he)
ow said she

(tiptop said he
don't stop said she
oh no said he)
go slow said she

(cccome?said he
ummm said she)
you're divine!said he
(you are Mine said she)

3

how

tinily
of

squir(two be
tween sto
nes)ming a gr

eenes
t you b
ecome

s whi
(mysterious
ly)te

one
t

hou

4

devil crept in eden wood
(grope me wonderful grope me good)
and he saw two humans roaming
—hear that tree agroaning

woman chewed and man he chewed
(open beautiful open good)
and their eyes were wet and shining
—feel that snake aclimbing

lord he called and angel stood
(poke me darling o poke me good)
with a big thick sword all flaming
—o my god i'm coming

5

moan
(is)
ing

the she of the
sea
un

der a who
a he a moon a
magic out

of the black this which of
one street leaps quick
squirmthicklying lu

minous night
mare som
e w

hereanynoevery
ing(danc)ing
wills&weres

6

youful

larger
of smallish)

Humble a
rosily
,nimblest;

c–urlin–g
noworld
Silent is

blue
(sleep!new

girlgold

she being Brand

-new;and you
know consequently a
little stiff i was
careful of her and(having

thoroughly oiled the universal
joint tested my gas felt of
her radiator made sure her springs were O.

K.)i went right to it flooded-the-carburetor cranked her

up,slipped the
clutch(and then somehow got into reverse she
kicked what
the hell)next
minute i was back in neutral tried and

again slo-wly;bare,ly nudg.   ing(my

lev-er Right-
oh and her gears being in
A 1 shape passed
from low through
second-in-to-high like
greasedlightning)just as we turned the corner of Divinity

avenue i touched the accelerator and give

her the juice,good

                    (it

was the first ride and believe i we was
happy to see how nice she acted right up to
the last minute coming back down by the Public
Gardens i slammed on

the
internalexpanding
&
externalcontracting
brakes Bothatonce and

brought allofher tremB
-ling
to a:dead.

stand-
;Still)

8

hips lOOsest OOping shoulders blonde& pastoral hair,strong,
arms and smelling of HAY
woman in a carotcoloured skin yellow face chipsofanger splayed
from GriNDing-mouth waist pulledup on oneside SHOWED her
sweaty corset.
                    eyeslike   smoky   idols

girl,iceblue hair huGe lips like orangepeels,waV ingagreat
tricolour
          yelling silently
                          cheery-nose square pash eyes splut
tering warench ofscarlet on right-breast legs
monumentally aPart
(Girl)flagstuck in her breasts. she bent her neck and bit It
jam mingIt deeper—pink—complexion tooth gone left side red
we epingeye s CHUBBY

their grey   hands tired of making   Death Probable

hairycheeks faces like hugestrawberries
                                    they pass a funeral in
silence and their branches had a terrible greenness

                          La Grève the Goddess
                                        tooth less
witches from Whose.gumsBurs !tthe
                          Cry

leather faces,crinkling with Ideal,the common,people
let-out of darkNess

9

Perhaps it was Myself sits down in this chair.   There were two chairs,in fact.
My fur-coat on.   Light one cigarette.   You
came her stalking straw-coloured body,cached with longness of kimona.

Myself got up out of a chair(there are two)say "Berthe" or something else.
Her Nudity seats Itself sharply beside.   New person. —The champagne is ex-
cellent sir.— so we are drinking a little,and talked gradually of the war
France death my prison,all pleasant things.   "Je m'occuperai tout particu-
lierement de vos colis".   and send one to The Zulu,as i want, one to mon
camarade   "vous n'avez pas trop chaud avec la pelisse?"no...I decline more
champagne anyway "Vous partez—?demain matin?""le train part a huit heures
un quart"

I watched her Flesh graciously destroy its cruel posture   "alors:il faut
bien dormir
".then is to be noticed...plural darkness spanked with singular light over
the pink
bed

To Undress—laughably mechanical   how my great ludicrous silent boots thrown
off Eye each other,really
As she lay:the body a flapping rag of life;I see pale whim of suppressed face
framed in the indignant hair,a jiggling rope of smile hung between painted
cheeks. and the furry rug of tongue where her Few teeth dance slowly like
bad women

My thumb smashes the world—
frot of furied eyes on brain!heart knotted with A suddenly nakedness—.

10

inthe,exquisite;

morning   sure   lyHer eye s exactly sit,ata little roundtable
among otherlittle roundtables   Her,eyes   count   slow(ly

obstre peroustimidi ties surElyfl)oat   iNg,the

ofpieces ofof sunligh tof fa l l in gof throughof treesOf.

(Fields Elysian

the like,a)slEEping neck a breathing a   ,lies
(slo wlythe wom an pa)ris her
flesh:wakes
              in little streets

while exactlygir lisHlegs;play;ing;nake;D
and

chairs wait under the trees

Fields slowly Elysian in
a firmcool-Ness   taxis, s.QuirM

and,   b etw ee nch air st ott er s thesillyold
WomanSellingBalloonS

In theex qui site

morning,
              her sureLyeye s sit-ex actly her sitsat a surely!little,
roundtable amongother;littleexactly round.   tables,

Her
    .eyes

II

ev erythingex Cept:

that
's what she's
got

—ex

cept what?
why
,what it

Takes.   now

you know(just as
well as i
do)what

it takes;& i don't mean It—

&
i don't
mean any

thing real

Ly what
;or ev
erythi

ng which.   but,

som
e
th

ing:Who

12

up into the silence the green
silence with a white earth in it

you will(kiss me)go

out into the morning the young
morning with a warm world in it

(kiss me)you will go

on into the sunlight the fine
sunlight with a firm day in it

you will go(kiss me

down into your memory and
a memory and memory

i)kiss me(will go)

13

if(you are i why certainly

the hour softly is
in all;places which move
seriously

Together.

let)us fold wholly ourselves smil-
ing because we love,
as doomed few alert(flowers and

excellently upon whom Night
wanders and wanders and)wanders
Or since,in air

like bubbles Faces
occur(shyly

to
one by bright
brief
one be)punc

-tured:the,green
nameless caterpillar of evening nib,ble,s
Solemnly a whitish leaf of sky.

through the tasteless minute efficient room
march hexameters of unpleasant
twilight,a twilight smelling of Vergil,
as me bang(to and from)
the huggering rags of white Latin flesh
which her body sometimes isn't
(all night,always,a warm incessant gush
of furious Paris flutters up the hill,
cries somethings laughters loves nothings float
upward,beautifully,forces crazily rhyme,
Montmartre s'amuse!obscure eyes hotly dote
....as awkwardly toward me for the millionth time
sidles the ruddy rubbish of her kiss
i taste upon her mouth cabs and taxis.

15

the dress was a suspicious madder,importing the cruelty of roses.
The exciting simplicity of her hipless body,pausing to invent im-
perceptible bulgings of the pretended breasts,forked in surpris-
able unliving eyes chopped by a swollen inanity of picture hat.

the arms hung ugly.,the hands sharp and impertinently dead.

expression began with the early cessation of her skirt.   flesh-
less melody of the,keenly lascivious legs.   painful ankles large
acute brutal feet propped on irrelevantly ferocious heels.

Her gasping slippery body moved with the hideous spontaneity
of a solemn mechanism.   beneath her drab tempo of hasteful futility
lived brilliantly the enormous rhythm of absurdity.

skin like the poisonous fragility of ice newly formed upon an old
pool.   Her nose was small,exact,stupid.   mouth normal,large,unclever.
hair genuinely artificial,unpleasantly tremendous.

under flat lusts of light her nice concupiscence appeared round-
ed.

if she were alive,death was amusing

16

her
flesh
Came
at

meassandca V
         ingint
                    oA
chute
     i had cement for her,
     merrily
we became each
other humped to tumbling

garble   when
a
minute
pulled the sluice

            emerging.

concrete

                                    i will be
      M o ving in the Street of her

bodyfee l inga ro undMe the traffic of
lovely;muscles-sinke x p i r i n   g S
            uddenl
      Y   totouch
                        the curvedship of
                                    Her-
....kIss   her:hands
                        will play on,mE as
dea d tunes OR s-crap p-y lea Ves flut te rin g
from Hideous trees or

         Maybe Mandolins
                        l oo k-
         pigeons fly ingand

whee(:are,SpRiN,k,LiNg an in-stant with sunLight
then)l-
ing all go BlacK wh-eel-ing

oh
   ver
         mYveRylitTle

street
where
you will come,

                  at twi li ght
      s(oon & there's
      a   m oo
)n.

18

i
(meet)t(touch)
ems crouch(
lunge
)ing bruiseD
Suddenly by thousand

starings rinsed with
thoroughly million yells they
f-oo-l(whom,blinds;blood)pa-nt
stab are

(slopped givers of not)bang
spurting mesh(faith
-ful which -ly try are ing)al

most fe(hug)males(one-t
wo-l oop-l

eftsthrowr ightsm issingupperc

uts-lurc hhurt-re
coil charge &)swooN

Crowdloomroar:ing;diskface,es
(are two
notSoft soft one are

hard one notHard)not
boys boy-
ish(a stopped A)with!notgirl'swith?dumb
(thewith girl)ness(ish The eyesthe

Is)aRe
iS ar(ise)wi
it(wit(hprettyw)ith)mr
jeff dick
son fec

i
(m
c)
t

(m
x
x

x
ii)

I

19

(swooning)a pillar of youngly

loveflesh topped
with danc
ing egghead strutstrolls

eager a(twice

by
Dizzying eyeplums
pun

ctured)moo

nface swimming
ly
dreamseems

(vivi

d
an O
of

milky tranceworld writhes

in
twi
nn

ingly scarlet woundsmile)

20

as
we lie side by side
my little breasts become two sharp delightful strutting towers and
i shove hotly the lovingness of my belly against you

your arms are
young;
your arms will convince me,in the complete silence speaking
upon my body
their ultimate slender language.

do not laugh at my thighs.

there is between my big legs a crisp city.
when you touch me
it is Spring in the city;the streets beautifully writhe,
it is for you;do not frighten them,
all the houses terribly tighten
upon your coming:
and they are glad
as you fill the streets of my city with children.

my love you are a bright mountain which feels.
you are a keen mountain and an eager island whose
lively slopes are based always in the me which is shrugging,which is
under you and around you and forever:i am the hugging sea.
O mountain you cannot escape me
your roots are anchored in my silence;therefore O mountain
skilfully murder my breasts,still and always

i will hug you solemnly into me.

21

first she like a piece of ill-oiled
machinery does a few naked tricks

next into unwhiteness,clumsily
lustful,plunges—covering the soiled
pillows with her violent hair
(eagerly then the huge greedily

Bed swallows easily our antics,
like smooth deep sweet ooze where
two guns lie,smile,grunting.)

"C'est la guerre"i probably suppose,
c'est la guerre busily hunting
for the valve which will stop this.
as i push aside roughly her nose

Hearing the large mouth mutter kiss pleece

22

love was—entire excellently steep

therefore(most deftly as tall dreams unleash
pale wish,between mirrors thoughts blundering
merge;softly thing forgets its name:
memories descending open—time reverses)
the million poets of our single flesh

gradually prepare to enter sleep

Around worldfully whom noises pour
carefully(exploding faintly)while(humbling

faintestly)among unminds go stumbling
cries bright whip-crash leaps lunge thundering
wheels and striving(are now faintestly)come
strutting such(wonderfully how through our

deepestly hearts immensely strolling)horses.

23

skies may be blue;yes
(when gone are hail and sleet and snow)
but bluer than my darling's eyes,
spring skies are no

hearts may be true;yes
(by night or day in joy or woe)
but truer than your lover's is,
hearts do not grow

nows may be new;yes
(as new as april's first hello)
but new as this our thousandth kiss,
no now is so

24

into a truly
curving form
enters my
soul

feels all small
facts dissolved
by the lewd guess
of fabulous immensity

the sky screamed
the sun died)
the ship lifts
on seas of iron

breathing height eating
steepness the
ship climbs
murmuring silver mountains

which
disappear(and
only
was night

and through only this night a
mightily form moves
whose passenger and whose
pilot my spirit is

25

the moon is hiding in
her hair.
The
lily
of heaven
full of all dreams,
draws down.

cover her briefness in singing
close her with intricate faint birds
by daisies and twilights
Deepen her,

Recite
upon her
flesh
the rain's

pearls singly-whispering.

"she had that softness which is falsity"
he frowned "plus budding strictly chasms of
uninnocence for eyes:and slippery
a pseudomind,not quite which could believe

in anything except most far from so
itself(with deep roots hugging fear's sweet mud
she floated on a silly nonworld's how
precarious inexistence like some dead

provocatively person of a thing
mancurious and manicured)i gave
the wandering stem a vivid(being young)
yank;and then vanished.   Seeing which,you dove

and brought me to the surface' smiling "by
my dick,which since has served me handily"

27

the dirty colours of her kiss have just
throttled
        my seeing blood,her heart's chatter

riveted a weeping skyscraper

in me

      i bite on the eyes' brittle crust
(only feeling the belly's merry thrust
Boost my huge passion like a business

and the Y her legs panting as they press

proffers its omelet of fluffy lust)
at six exactly
        the alarm tore

two slits in her cheeks.   A brain peered at the dawn.
she got up

       with a gashing yellow yawn
and tottered to a glass bumping things.
she picked wearily something from the floor

Her hair was mussed,and she coughed while tying strings

28

O It's Nice To Get Up In,the slipshod mucous kiss
of her riant belly's fooling bore
—When The Sun Begins To(with a phrasing crease
of hot subliminal lips,as if a score
of youngest angels suddenly should stretch neat necks
just to see how always squirms
the skilful mystery of Hell)me suddenly

grips in chuckles of supreme sex.

In The Good Old Summer Time.
My gorgeous bullet in tickling intuitive flight
aches,just,simply,into,her.   Thirsty
stirring.   (Must be summer.   Hush.   Worms.)
But It's Nicer To Lie In Bed
       —eh?   I'm

not.   Again.   Hush.   God.   Please hold.   Tight

LANGUAGE
EXPERIMENTS

The orthographical inventions—altered spellings, irregular use of lower case, and so on—are expansions of the ancient poetic method of connotation, where a single word is pressed for richness latent in it.
—John Logan, "The Organ-Grinder and the Cockatoo" (1970)

While it is commonly understood that no other early modern poet experimented as wildly with language, what is not so well known is the degree of Cummings' departures. He took apart the materials of poetry, initially familiar words and punctuation marks, and then put them together in unfamiliar and striking ways. This selection includes his most extreme poetic experiments. Look for expressive capitalizations, verbal fragmentation and compression, neologisms, cunning repunctuation, lines both abbreviated and extended, representational typography, foreign vocabularies, dialect, and variation within repetition. To measure what these add to his writing, simply consider that the opening selection here contains the following words:

moon over towns moon whisperless creature huge gropingness
who perfectly who float newly alone is dreamest only the moon
over towns slowly sprouting spirit

And then see what Cummings did to this text. Though such
devices become a principal content of many of these poems,
note that the poem beginning "16 heures" is a satire of Parisian
policing.

mOOn Over tOwns mOOn
whisper
less creature huge grO
pingness

whO perfectly whO
flOat
newly alOne is
dreamest

oNLY THE MooN o
VER ToWNS
SLoWLY SPRoUTING SPIR
IT

2

nouns to nouns

wan
wan

too nons too

and
and

nuns two nuns

w an d
ering

in sin

g
ular untheknowndulous s

pring

3

in Just-
spring   when the world is mud-
luscious the little
lame balloonman

whistles   far   and wee

and eddieandbill come
running from marbles and
piracies and it's
spring

when the world is puddle-wonderful

the queer
old balloonman whistles
far   and   wee
and bettyandisbel come dancing

from hop-scotch and jump-rope and

it's
spring
and
     the

          goat-footed

balloonMan   whistles
far
and
wee

4

Lord John Unalive(having a fortune of fifteengrand
£
thanks to the socalled fact that maost faolks rally demannd canned
saounds)
gloats
upon the possession of quotes keltyer close
" "

aureally(yawning while all the dominoes)fall:down;in,rows

5

moon over gai
-té.a
sharp crone dodders be-
tween taxis swirl hues crowds mov
-ing ing ing
among who dreams whom mutterings dream &

:the moon over death over edgar the
moon
        over smellings of gently smell of deads
(lovers grip sprawl twitch lovers)
& one dog?piglike big!sorrows

always;finally and always,the iflike moon over moving
me—the
moon
m
ov—in

g
over(moving)you beautifully also;at

denfert the fat strongman has put
down his carpet from which rise slim curving mighty
children while a python over the way freezes
a serpent becomes a
rod smiles
the liontamer nearby hieroglyphs
soar dip
dip
soar equalling noise solemn

dolls re
-volve whirlswans rabbitsare:
swimswim
painted-with-horses-with-painted-
with eyes and the.m

oon over juillet moon over s
-unday

O:
m
o
o
n
o
 (ver no(w ove(r all;
                    o
ver pinkthisgreen acr)o)greenthatpink)
acrobata

mong
trees climbing on
A

pi llarofch airso vertheseu pstareth oseings
over
(a hard a
hard a girl a girl)sing
-ing ing(ing
sing)ing a soft a song a softishsongly

v
  o
   i
    c
     e o
        ver
(whi!tethatr?apidly
legthelessne sssuc kedt oward
black,this

)roUnd ingrOundIngly rouNdar(round)ounDing
                             ;ball
                             balll
                             ballll
                             balllll

6

go(perpe)go

(tu)to(al
adve

nturin
g p
article

s of s
ini
sterd
exte

ri)go to(ty)the(om
nivorou salways lugbrin
g ingseekfindlosin g
motilities
are)go to

the
ant
(al
ways

alingwaysing)
go to the ant thou go
(inging)

to the
ant,thou ant–

eater

life hurl my
yes,crumbles hand(ful released conarefetti)ev eryflitter,inga. where
mil(lions of aflickf)litter ing brightmillion ofS hurl;edindodg:ing
whom areEyes shy-dodge is bright cruMbshandful,quick-hurl edinwho
Is flittercrumbs,fluttercrimbs are floatfallin,g;allwhere:
a:crimbflitteringish is arefloatsis ingfallalll!mil,shy milbrightlions
my(hurl flicker handful
in)dodging are shybrigHteyes is crum bs(alll)if,ey Es

8

brIght

bRight s??? big
(soft)

soft near calm
(Bright)
calm st?? holy

(soft briGht deep)
yeS near sta? calm star big yEs
alone
(wHo

Yes
near deep whO big alone soft near
deep calm deep
????Ht ?????T)
Who(holy alone)holy(alone holy)alone

9

           cont)-
in
   this
           crazily
per
c
  hedtown(screams a
& screams
)&
screams
A
n(about to
bring for
           t)hW
omb
an
   -(in
u,
all;
y:

logeorge
     lo
         wellifitisn't eddy   how's the boy
grandhave youheard
            shoot

                  you knowjim
goodscout   well

   married

   the hellyousay
        whoto

     'member ritagail
   do i remember rita   what'sthejoke

                well

                      goddam

    don'ttakeit too hard old boy

sayare you kidding   me   because ifyouare   byhell
  easyall george   watchyourstep old fellow

   christ

     that   that

mut

sh estiffl
ystrut sal
lif san
dbut sth

epouting(gWh.ono:w
s li psh ergo
wnd ow n,
                    r
Eve

aling 2 a
-sprout eyelands)sin
uously&them&twi
tching,begins

unununun?
butbutbut??
   tonton??
ing????

—Out-&
            steps;which
flipchucking
.grins
gRiNdS

d is app ea r in gly
eyes grip live loop croon mime
nakedly hurl asquirm the
dip&giveswoop&swoon&ingly

seethe firm swirl hips whirling climb to
GIVE
(yoursmine mineyours yoursmine
!
i( )t)

12

this(that

grey)white
(man)horse

floats
on 4
3rdtoes

p
(drooli
ngly supp
ort 2 be

nt
toothpick
s)

ro
ude

stly(stuck in a spanked behind

o pr
gress verily thou art m
mentous superc
lossal hyperpr
digious etc i kn
w & if you d

n't why g
  to yonder s
called newsreel s
called theatre & with your
wn eyes beh

ld The
            (The president The
            president of The president
            of the The)president of

            the(united The president of the
            united states The president of the united
            states of The President Of The)United States

            Of America unde negant redire quemquam supp
sedly thr
w
  i
    n
      g
        a
          b
            aseball

14

ondumonde"

(first than caref
ully;pois
edN-o wt he
n
,whysprig
        sli

nkil
 -Y-
   strol(pre)ling(cise)dy(ly)na(
   mite)

    :yearnswoons;

      &Isdensekil-
        ling-whipAlert-floatScor
        ruptingly)

                ça-y-est
                droppe5
                qu'est-ce que tu veux
                Dwrith
                il est trop fort le nègre
                esn7othingish8s
                c'est fini
                pRaW,lT;O:
              allons

           9
           &

           .

              (musically-who?

        pivoting)
          SmileS

        "ahlbrhoon

15

swi(
    across!gold's

rouNdly
)ftblac
kl(ness)y

a–motion–upo–nmotio–n

Less?
    thE
(against
is
)Swi

mming

(w–a)s
bIr

d,

16

lis
-ten

you know what i mean when
the first guy drops you know
everybody feels sick or
when they throw in a few gas
and the oh baby shrapnel
or my feet getting dim freezing or
up to your you know what in water or
with the bugs crawling right all up
all everywhere over you all me everyone
that's been there knows what
i mean a god damned lot of
people don't and never
never
will know,
they don't want

to
no

17

it's jolly
odd what pops into
your jolly tête when the
jolly shells begin dropping jolly fast you
hear the rrmp and
then nearerandnearerandNEARER
and before
you can

!

& we're

NOT
(oh—
—i say

that's jolly odd
old thing,jolly
odd,jolly
jolly odd isn't
it jolly odd.

18

16 heures
l'Etoile

the communists have fine Eyes

some are young some old none
look alike the flics rush
batter the crowd sprawls collapses
singing knocked down trampled the kicked by
flics rush(the

Flics,tidiyum,are
very tidiyum reassuringly similar,
they all have very tidiyum
mustaches,and very
tidiyum chins,and just above
their very tidiyum ears their
very tidiyum necks begin)
                              let us add

that there are 50(fifty)flics for every
one(1)communist and
all the flics are very organically
arranged
and their nucleus(composed
of captains in freshly-creased
-uniforms with only-just-
shined buttons
tidiyum
before and behind)has a nucleolus:

the Prefect of Police

(a dapper derbied
creature,swaggers daintily
twiddling
his tiny cane
and,mazurkas about tweak-
ing his wing collar pecking at his im

-peccable cravat directing being
shooting his cuffs
saluted everywhere saluting
reviewing processions of minions
tappingpeopleontheback

"allezcirculez")

—my   he's brave....
the
communists pick
up themselves friends
& their hats legs &

arms brush dirt coats
smile looking hands
spit blood teeth

the Communists have(very)fine eyes
(which stroll hither and thither through the
evening in bruised narrow questioning faces)

19

Among

>   these
>   red pieces of
> day(against which and
> quite silently hills
> made of blueandgreen paper

scorchbend ingthem
-selves-U
pcurv E,into:
>   anguish(clim
> b)ing
> s-p-i-r-a-
> l
>   and,disappear)
>   Satanic and blasé

a black goat lookingly wanders

There is nothing left of the world but
into this noth
ing il treno per
Roma si-gnori?
jerk.
ilyr,ushes

20

,mean-
hum
a)now

(nit
y unb
uria

ble fore(hurry
into
heads are
legs think wrists

argue)short(eyes do
bang hands angle
scoot bulbs marry a become)
ened
(to is

see!so
long door
golf slam bridge train shriek
chewing whistles hugest
to
morrow from smiles sin

k
ingly ele
vator glide pinn
)pu(
acle to

rubber)tres(plants how grin
ho)cen(tel
und
ead the

not stroll
living spawn imitate)ce(re
peat

credo fais do
do neighbours re babies
                    while:

ta
ppin
g
toe

hip
popot
amus Back

gen
teel–ly
lugu-
bri ous

eyes
LOOPTHELOOP

as

fathandsbangrag

fl

a
tt
ene

d d

reaml
essn
esse

s wa

it
sp
i

t)(t

he
s
e

f

ooli
sh sh
apes

ccocoucougcoughcoughi

ng with me
n more o
n than in the

m

23

grEEn's d

an
cing on hollow was

young Up
floatingly clothes tumbledish
olD(with

sprouts o
ver and)a–
live
wanders remembe

r
.
ing per
F
ectl
y

crumb
ling eye
–holes oUt of whe
reful whom(leas

tly)
smiles the
infinite nothing

of
M

an

24

warped this perhapsy
stumbl
i
 NgflounderpirouettiN
                    g

:seized(

tatterdemalion
dow
     nupfloatsw
                oon
InG

s ly)tuck.s its(ghostsoul sheshape)

elf into leasting forever most
magical maybes of certainly
never the iswas

teetertiptotterish

sp-
   inwhirlpin
              -wh
EEling
;a!who,

(

whic hbubble ssomethin
gabou tlov
e)

25

thethe
the pink

Tartskids with
thecas-tanets
in5/4; Time

      chick.chick
but:that Mat isse like

-with-the-chinese-eyebrowsMan
gave me,A,

(peach
    a soft eyes syriansang asong tohim self
all

about the desertbyIt self
             while) nextto
Mesmoked eleven camels
         !

and i got a Bad almond
chick.
    thepinkisht artskiDs...

    with thema Tiss eeyeb Rowspeach es
a soft desert smoked bad me whilepin Kishcam elscasta?netsits
Elf
  allaBout .

      (chic)
        -kchi

cK,

26

applaws)

"fell
ow
sit
isn'ts"

(a paw s

27

(fea
therr
ain

:dreamin
g field o
ver forest &;

wh
o could
be

so
!f!
te

r?n
oo
ne)

28

sunset)edges become swiftly
corners(Besides
which,i note how
fatally toward

twilight the a little
tilted streets spill lazily
multitudes out of final

towers;captured:in
the narrow light

of

inverno)this
is the season of
crumbling & folding
hopes,hark;feet(fEEt
f-e-e-t-noWheregoingaLwaYS

29

&(all during the

dropsin
king god my sic
kly a thingish o crashdis
appearing con ter fusion ror collap
sing thatthis is whichwhat yell itfulls o
f cringewiltdroolery i
mean really th
underscream of sudde
nly perishing eagerly everyw
here shutting forever&forever fol
ding int
o absolute gone &
positive quite n
ever & bi
g screeching new black perfectly isn

't)one rose opened

30

An(fragrance)Of

(Begins)
millions

Of Tints(and)
&
(grows)Slowly(slowly)Voyaging

tones intimate tumult
(Into)bangs
minds into
dream(An)quickly

Not

un deux trois
der
    die

Stood(apparition.)
WITH(THE ROUND AIR IS FILLED)OPENING

innerly

UningstrolL
(stamens&pistil
                silent
A s groupingThe
6around one
darks to 7th s
            o howpale)
bluedmufFletomben

                    outerly

jeT
ting lip ssixs ting
sWervesca
rletlycaR v Ingharness
Of
curvish(

            ,males await she
patiently 1

)littlecrownGrave
whose whorlclown of spreadnessed bE
rich from-soft quits(now)ly
Comes;
:lush
ly-smootHdumb droopnew-gree

N.lyestmostsaresl e A v e S

32

it)It will it
Will come(we
being
unwound & gone into the ground)but

though

with wormS eyes
writhe amor(Though through

our hearts hugely squirm
roots)us
        ly;though
hither nosing lymoles cru.Ising

thither:t,ouch soft-ly me and eye(you
leSs

)ly(un
        der the mi
                croscopic world's

whens,wheels;wonders:
murders.cries:hopes;
houses,clouds.kisses,
lice;headaches:ifs.

)
 yet shall
our Not to
be

deciphered
selves

merely Continue to experience

a neverish subchemistry of
alWays
)fiercely live whom on

Large Darkness And The Middle Of
The
E

a
r
t
H

33

twi-
    is -Light bird
ful
-ly dar
kness eats

a distance a
c(h)luck
(l)ing of just bells (touch)ing
?mind

(moon begins The
)
now,est hills er dream;new
.oh if

      when:
&
a
nd O impercept i bl

34

chas sing does(who
,ins
tead,
smiles alw

ays a trifl
e
w
hile ironin

g!
nob odyknowswhos esh
?i
rt)n't

35

if the

green
opens
a little a
little
was
much and much
is

too if

the green robe
o
p
e
n
s
and two are

wildstrawberries

36

goo–dmore–ning(en

ter)nize–aday(most
gently herculanean

my mortal)yoo

make sno eye kil
yoo(friend the laughing
grinning)we

no(smiling)strike

agains
De Big Boss
(crying)jew wop
rich poor(sing

ing)

He
    no
        care
            so
                what

yoo–gointa–doo?(ice

coal wood
man)nic
he like
wint–air

nic like ot–am

sum-air(young
old nic)
like spring yoo

un–air–stan?me

crazy
me like

evry-ting

37

a thrown a

-way It
with some-
thing sil
-very

;bright,&:mys(

a thrown a-
way
X
-mas)ter-

i

-ous wisp A of glo-
ry.pr
-ettily
cl(tr)in(ee)gi-

ng

38

says ol man no body—
datz woty say
yez,honey
But
we don't care an
we'll just sing:O
Sumpn
ter Sumpn an
lipster
lips ahmindy
OuterCo
ro
naofyohr
SolarE
clipse

39

un(bee)mo

vi
n(in)g
are(th
e)you(o
nly)

asl(rose)eep

40

that melancholy

fellow'll play
his handorgan
until you say

"i want a fortune"

.At which(smiling)he stops:
& pick
ing up a magical stick
t,a,p,s

this dingy cage:then with a ghost

's rainfaint windthin
voice-which-is
no-voice sobcries

"paw?lee"

—whereupon out(SlO
wLy)steps(to
mount the wand)a by no
means almost

white morethanPerson;who

(riding through space
to diminutive this
opened drawer)tweak

S with his brutebeak

one fatal faded(pinkish or
yellowish maybe)piece
of pitiful paper—
but now,as Mr bowing Cockatoo

proffers the meaning of the stars

14th st dis(because my tears
are full of eyes)appears.   Because
only the truest things always

are true because they can't be true

41

who is this
dai
   nty
mademoiselle

the o
    f her
luminous
se
  lf
a shy(an

if a
    whis
per a where
a hidi
      ng)est

meta
ph
  or
?la lune

42

!

o(rounD)moon,how
do
you(rouNd
er
than roUnd)float;
who
lly &(rOunder than)
go
:ldenly(Round
est)

?

43

& sun &

sil
e
nce
e

very

w
here
noon
e

is exc

ep
t
on
t

his

b
oul
der
a

drea(chipmunk)ming

44

ardensteil-henarub-izabeth)

this noN
allgotupfittokill
She with the
& how

p-e-r-f-e-c-t-l-y-d-e-a-d

Unvoice(which frightenS
a noisy most
park's
least timorous pigeons)squ

-I-

nts(while showe
ring cigaretteash O
ver that scre
Amingfeeblyoff

s,p;r:i;n,g

45

n

ot eth
eold almos
tladyf eebly
hurl ing
cr u

mb

son ebyo
neatt wothre
efourfi ve&six
engli shsp
arr ow

s

46

f

  eeble a blu
r of cr
umbli
ng m

oo

  n(
poor shadoweaten
was
of is and un of

so

)h
   ang
   s
   from

thea lmo st mor ning

47

s.tiːrst;hiso,nce;maːn

c
ollapse
d

.iːns;unli,gh;t:

"ah
gwonyuhdoanfool
me"

toitselfw.hispering

48

a gr

eyhaire
d(m
utteri
ng)bab
yfa

ced

dr(lun
g)u
(ing)
nk g

RowL

(eyeaintu)
s
(hfraiduh

nOHw

u
n)

!

49

a he as o
ld as who stag
geri
ng up some streetfu

l of peopl
e lurche
s viv
idly

from ti(& d
esperate
ly)m
e to ti

me shru
gg
ing as if to say b
ut for chreyesake how ca

n
i s
ell drunk if i
be pencils

50

who(at

her nons-
elf
's unself too
-thf-
ully lee
-r-

ing)can this plati

-num fl-
oozey
begin to(a
-lm-
ost)imagi
-n-

e she is

51

(hills chime with thrush)

A
hummingbird princess
FlOaTs
doll-angel-life
from

Bet:To;Bouncing,Bet

the
ruby&emerald zigging
HE
of a zagflash king
poUnc

es buzzsqueaking th

ey
tangle in twitter
y t
wofroing chino
ise

r(!)i(?)e(.)s

52

e
cco the uglies
t

s
ub
sub

urba
n skyline on earth between whose d
owdy

hou
se
s

l
ooms an eggyellow smear of wintry sunse
t

53

insu nli gh t

o
verand
o
vering

A

onc
eup
ona
tim

e ne wsp aper

54

l(a

le
af
fa

ll

s)
one
l

iness

55

as if as

if a mys
teriouSly("i am alive"

)
 brave

ly and(th
e moon's al-down)most whis
per(here)ingc r O

wing;ly:cry.be,gi N s agAains

t b
ecomin
gsky?t r e e s
!

m ore&(o uto f)mor e torn(f og r

e
elingwhiRls)are pouring rush fields drea
mf(ull

        y

          are.)
&
som

ewhereishbudofshape

now,s
tI
r
ghost

?s

tirf lic;k
e rsM-o
:ke(c.
    l

i,

m
  !
b
)& it:s;elf,

mmamakmakemakesWwOwoRworLworlD

VISUAL POETRY
AND
SOUND POETRY

By 1935, when his No Thanks *appeared, Cummings was as visually sophisticated as anybody who has ever worked in the field. No longer were his effects limited to visual onomatopoeia, or just one step from it; that is, no longer did he use visual devices merely to illustrate something already denoted; he used them to supply content which would not otherwise have existed.*

—Bob Grumman, Of Manywhere-at-Once *(1990)*

It is scarcely surprising that the most experimental major poet of his generation should have broached visual poetry, among other veins since more elaborately mined. He composed words in various images, beginning with that of rain (echoing Guillaume Apollinaire) and including Constantin Brancusi's sculpture. Many shapes are his own invention, customarily within the painterly convention of making a single image (rather than a sequence). On pages 144 and 145 there are two poems, different visualizations of the same language, that in the *Complete Poems* (1991) appear 873 pages apart. And on page 148 there is one of the visual poems that Richard S. Kennedy discovered in the course of producing his biography of E. E. Cummings, *Dreams in the Mirror* (1980). This one, in particular, strikes me as quite successful and worth reprinting here. The selection here also includes the famous "grasshopper" poem in instructive French, Italian, Portuguese, German, Dutch, Polish, and Russian translations along with the original. Even though he could have added drawings to his words, Cummings remained a mediumistic purist. Several decades ago, he composed wholly linguistic texts whose principal enhancements are acoustic, rather than, say, syntactical. While there was no term for such writing then, now it is called sound poetry.

l

n w
O
h
S
LoW
h
myGODye
s s

2

air,

be
comes
or

(a)

new
(live)
now

;&

th
(is no littler
th

an a:

fear no bigger
th
an a

hope)is

st
anding
st

a.r

3

b
et
wee
n no
w dis
appear
ing mou
ntains a
re drifti
ng christi
an how swee
tliest bell
s and we'l
l be you'
ll be i'
ll be ?
? ther
efore
let'
s k
is
s

4

the
   sky
      was
can dy lu
minous
       edible
spry
    pinks shy
lemons
greens coo l choc
olate
s.

 un der,
 a lo
co
mo
   tive   s pout
         ing
          vi
          o
         lets

5

          the sky
          was   can dy
     lu   mi
          nous   ed
                          i
          ble
              spry   pinks
              shy   lem
          ons
                                greens

       cool
     choco   lates
          un   der
  a   lo
        co
        mo   tive   s pout
                        ing
              vi
        o   lets

6

                you
             in win
           ter who sit
          dying thinking
         huddled behind dir
        ty glass mind muddled
       and cuddled by dreams(or some
      times vacantly gazing through un
     washed panes into a crisp todo of
      murdering uncouth faces which pass rap
     idly with their breaths.)"people are walking deaths
    in this season" think "finality lives up
   on them a little more openly than usual
  hither,thither who briskly busily carry the as
 tonishing & spontaneous & difficult ugliness
  of themselves with a more incisive simplicity a
   more intensively brutal futility"And sit
    huddling dumbly behind three or two partly tran
     sparent panes which by some loveless trick sepa
      rate one stilled unmoving mind from a hun
       dred doomed hurrying brains(by twos
        or threes which fiercely rapidly
         pass with their breaths)in win
          ter you think,die slow
           ly "toc tic" as i
            have seen trees(in
             whose black bod
              ies leaves
               hide

7

tw

o o
ld
o

nce upo

n
a(
n

o mo

re
)time
me

n

sit(l
oo
k)dre

am

two   brass   buttons   off
your   scar let   coatlo
             ret   taone   old   dint
             ed   and
a   new   one
you   don't   re
                    mem
          ber
you   were   drunk
                    when
i   askedret   ta   for   the
                                             rose   in
          her   hair
     you   can't   havethatshe
smiled   lar   riehe
                                                give   methe
     bloom
aint   itpretty
                              but   kid
     you   gut
a
knife   yes   op'   nit   thanks
my   teeth
     aint   strong   it's   the
          booze   gets   'im   and   she
                                                        hands methe
          two   brass   buttons
                    nev
          er   drink
dear

                    r-p-o-p-h-e-s-s-a-g-r
                who
        a)s w(e loo)k
        upnowgath
                PPEGORHRASS
                            eringint(o-
            aThe):l
                eA
                    !p:
    S   a
                        (r
        rIvInG   .gRrEaPsPhOs)
                                        to
        rea(be)rran(com)gi(e)ngly
        ,grasshopper;

10

e-r-e-l-l-e-t-u-s-a

qui

sou)s n(os yeu)x
sevoilàramass

LLESREAUTE

antpou(r

unLe):b

oN

!d:

It

a

(r

rIvAnT   .sEaLuLeEtR)

pour

réa(de)rran(veni)gea(r)mment
,sauterelle;

Translation into French by D. Jon Grossman

a-t-l-e-t-l-a-v-c-a
                    che
me)n tr(e guar)d
iamoinsusi
          VALLETTACA
                              forma(n–
El):s
      Al
        !t:
O   a
                    (r
rIvAndO   .cAtTaValLe)
                              per
ri(di)com(veni)por(re)si
,cavalletta;

Translation into Italian by Mary de Rachewiltz

12

o-h-o-t-n-a-f-g-a

que

s)e e(u olh)o
paraoaltor
      HOTGOAFAN
                   eunindose(n–
umEle:s
     aL
        !t:

A   c
          (h
eGaNdO   .gOaTfOaNh)
                                  a
recom(tor)pon(n)d(ar–se)o
,gafanhoto;

Translation into Portuguese by Augusto de Campos

152

13

<pre>
                    r-ü-p-f-e-s-a-g-h-r
              der
wi)e wi)r hinseh)n
sichhochjetzt
        PFEGÜRHRAS
                        raff(t-
zum):s
      prU
         !ng:
                                und
              (auf
sEtzT   .gRraPfeHüs)
                                um
sich(wie)zu(der)ord(zum)nen
,grashüpfer;
</pre>

Translation into German by Eva Hesse

153

14

r-h-i-p-n-a-s-k-a-n
                die
n)u w(e op)kij
kenzichopmaa
        NPINAKHRAS
                        ktto(t-
otDe):s
        pRO
            !ng:
EN   n
                (ee
    RkOmT   .kHnApRiAns)
                            om te
herg(wor)roep(de)ere(n)nderwijze
,sprinkhaan;

Translation into Dutch by Peter Verstegen

15

k-o-i-k-n-i-s-p-a

który

g)dy sp(oglądam)y
powyżejustawi

ONIPKKASI

ającg(o

wTo):s

kA

!cz:

E   i

(r

oBiSiĘzEń   .pKaIsNkOi)

w

odm(porz)ie(ądk)nn(u)ym
,pasikonik ;

Translation into Polish by Stanisław Baranczak

155

16

* * *

                                        (р-к-ч-е-с-в-о

                        которое

ка)к м(ы види)м
приготавли

                        ЧЕОКРВС

                                в (а-
еТСя):п!р

            ыг

                а

еТ   что-

                    (бы

вот-   . ВеРсКоЧ

                                            вот

перегр(превр)уппир(ат)ова(и)ться в
: сверчок;

Translation into Russian by Vladimir Britanishsky

17

wanta
spendsix

dollars Kid
        2 for the room
and
        four   for the girl
thewoman wasnot

quite Fourteen   till she smiled
                      then

Centuries   she
            soft ly

repeated
well   whadyas ay
        dear
        wan
        taspend

    six

Dollars

18

o

the round
little man we
loved so isn't

no!w

a gay of a
brave and
a true of a

who have

r
olle
d i

nt

o
n
o

w(he)re

19

one

t
hi
s

snowflake

(a
  li
    ght
  in
g)

is upon a gra

v
es
t

one

20

SNOW

cru
  is
    ingw Hi
sperf
    ul
lydesc

BYS FLUTTERFULLY IF

(endbegi ndesginb ecend)tang
lesp
    ang
le
  s
    ofC omeg o

CRINGE WITHS

lilt(
   -ing-
      lyful
of)!
   (s
r

BIRDS BECAUSE AGAINS

emarkable
       s)h?
          y & a
             (from n
o(into whe)re f
         ind)
nd
   ArE

GLIB SCARCELYEST AMONGS FLOWERING

21

the(oo)is

lOOk
(aliv
e)e
yes

are(chIld)and

wh(g
o
ne)
o

w(A)a(M)s

22

nonsun blob a
cold to
skylessness
sticking fire

my are your
are birds our all
and one gone
away the they

leaf of ghosts some
few creep there
here or on
unearth

23

bingbongwhom chewchoo
laugh dingle nails personally
bung loamhome picpac
obviously scratches tomorrowlobs

wholeagainst you gringlehow
exudes thursday fasters
by button of whisper sum blinked
he belowtry eye nowbrow

sangsung née whitermuch grab
sicksilk soak sulksuck whim
poke if inch dimmer twist on
permament and slap tremendous

sorrydaze bog triperight
election who so thumb o'clock
asters miggle dim a ram
flat hombre sin bangaroom

slim guesser goose pin yessir wheel
no sendwisp ben jiffyclaus
bug fainarain wee celibate
amaranth clutch owch

so chuck slop hight evolute
my eerily oh gargle
to jip hug behemoth
truly pseudo yours podia

of radarw leschin

floatfloafloflf
lloloa
tatoatloatf loat fl oat
f loatI ngL

y

&fris
klispin
glyT
   w
     irlEric

,

t,
;d
; :a:
nC.eda:Nci;ddaanncciinn

(GIY)

a
 nda
    n–saint
dance!Dan
Sai ntd anc

&e&

—cupidoergosum
spun=flash
omiepsicronlonO—
megaeta?
      p
       aul D–as–in–tip–toe r

apeR

25

(b
  eLl
     s?
       bE

-ginningly(come-swarm:faces
ar;rive go.faces a(live)
sob bel
ls

(pour wo
       (things)
             men
                 selves-them

inghurl)bangbells(yawnchurches
suck people)reel(dark-
ly(whirling
in

(b
  ellSB
      el
       Ls)

-to sun(crash).Streets
glit
ter
a,strut:do;colours;are:m,ove

o im
    -pos-
       sibl
          y

(ShoutflowereD
flowerish boom
b el Lsb El l
s!cry)

(be
   llsbe
       lls)
         b
          (be
            llsbell)
                 ells
                   (sbells)

TEXTS SET
TO MUSIC

When [Erik Satie] threw his little closet pieces in the face of traditional concert music, they assumed the proportions of manifestoes: poster music. Thus intimacy becomes a public act. Satie's musique de placard conveys the same public privacy or private publicity as the drawings of Paul Klee and poems of E. E. Cummings.
— *Roger Shattuck,* The Banquet Years *(1958)*

In his entry on E. E. Cummings in *The New Grove Dictionary of American Music* (1986), the *New Yorker* critic Paul Griffiths notes, "Among the more than 200 settings of Cummings' verse, the poems most frequently set have been 'in just,' 'hist whist,' 'I thank you God for this most amazing,' 'sweet spring is your,' and 'tumbling hair.' " Griffiths attributes Cummings' popularity to his "sensitivity to phonetic values [that] made his writing a valuable starting-point for new approaches to text-setting." Another factor to consider is the poems that are esthetically similar to advanced music, which Cummings had assimilated, thanks to his acquaintance with Foster Damon, as early as his Harvard years. (Consider, by contrast, how the songs of the Second Vienna School— most notably Arnold Schoenberg, Alban Berg, and Anton von Webern—are compromised by old-fashioned expressionist verse.) To illustrate the various ways in which Cummings texts have been used, this section reprints opening pages of scores by John Cage, David Diamond, Peter Dickinson, Morton Feldman, and Peter Schickele alongside the Cummings poems they used. (Those wanting to get the entire scores or perform the works are advised to contact the publishers acknowledged on the copyright page.) At the end of this section is the passage from Cummings' *The Enormous Room* (1922) that the American composer David Diamond incorporated into his score of his 1948 piece of the same name, acknowledging Cummings' text without actually quoting from it. In the notes accompanying a 1992 recording of this work, Diamond adds, "If the text just quoted establishes the opening mood of the work, the following passage from the end of the novel fulfills the inevitability of the music's closing measure: '[T]hings new and curious and hard and strange and vibrant and immense, lifting with a great undulous stride firmly into immortal sunlight.' " From writing like that can music indeed be made.

1

i shall imagine life
is not worth dying,if
(and when)roses complain
their beauties are in vain

but though mankind persuades
itself that every weed's
a rose,roses(you feel
certain)will only smile

Setting by David Diamond

To Sibley and Hildegarde Watson
in memory of
Edward Estlin Cummings

I Shall Imagine Life

E. E. CUMMINGS
(1894–1962)

DAVID DIAMOND
(1962)

170

2

wherelings whenlings
(daughters of ifbut offspring of hopefear
sons of unless and children of almost)
never shall guess the dimension of

him whose
each
foot likes the
here of this earth

whose both
eyes
love
this now of the sky

—endlings of isn't
shall never
begin
to begin to

imagine how(only are shall be were
dawn dark rain snow rain
-bow &
a

moon
's whis-
per
in sunset

or thrushes toward dusk among whippoorwills or
tree field rock hollyhock forest brook chickadee
mountain.   Mountain)
whycoloured worlds of because do

not stand against yes which is built by
forever & sunsmell
(sometimes a wonder
of wild roses

sometimes)
with north
over
the barn

Setting by John Cage

FOREVER AND SUNSMELL

WORDS FROM A POEM BY
E. E. CUMMINGS

MUSIC BY
JOHN CAGE

duration: 5 minutes

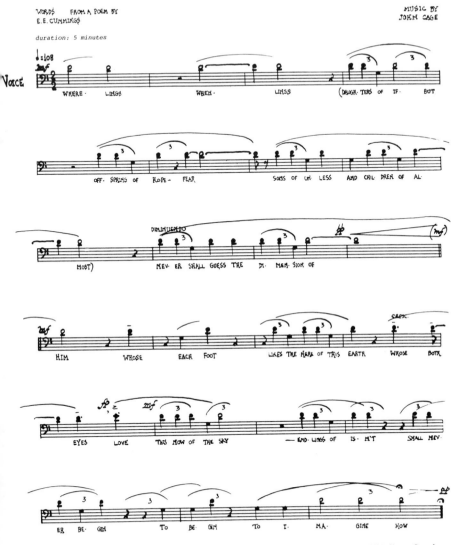

173

3

!blac
k
agains
t

(whi)

te sky
?t
rees whic
h fr

om droppe

d

,
le
af

a:;go

e
s wh
IrlI
n

.g

Setting by Morton Feldman

174

4 SONGS TO e. e. CUMMINGS (VOICE, CELLO, PIANO)

Morton Feldman

I

1.

4

why did you go
little fourpaws?
you forgot to shut
your big eyes.

where did you go?
like little kittens
are all the leaves
which open in the rain.

little kittens who
are called spring,
is what we stroke
maybe asleep?

do you know?or maybe did
something go away
ever so quietly
when we weren't looking.

Setting by John Cage

FIVE SONGS
for Contralto

e.e. cummings

John Cage

1. little four paws

Edition Peters 6710

5

dim
i
nu
tiv

e this park is e
mpty(everyb
ody's elsewher
e except me 6 e

nglish sparrow
s)a
utumn & t
he rai

n
th
e
raintherain

Setting by Peter Schickele

2. dim / l(a

NOTE: underlined consonants are to be held instead of the vowels that precede them.

6

it is at moments after i have dreamed
of the rare entertainment of your eyes,
when(being fool to fancy)i have deemed

with your peculiar mouth my heart made wise;
at moments when the glassy darkness holds

the genuine apparition of your smile
(it was through tears always)and silence moulds
such strangeness as was mine a little while;

moments when my once more illustrious arms
are filled with fascination,when my breast
wears the intolerant brightness of your charms:

one pierced moment whiter than the rest

—turning from the tremendous lie of sleep
i watch the roses of the day grow deep.

Setting by John Cage

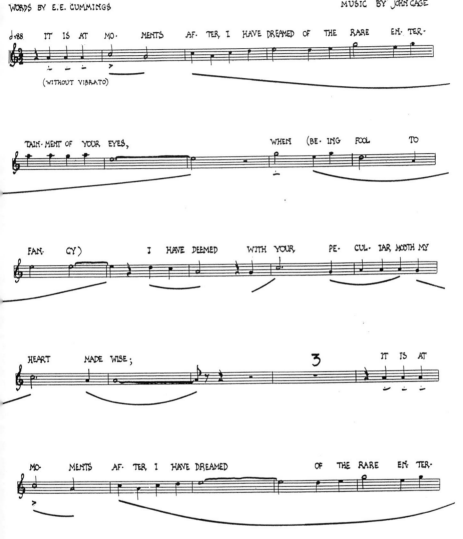

7

i thank You God for most this amazing
day:for the leaping greenly spirits of trees
and a blue true dream of sky;and for everything
which is natural which is infinite which is yes

(i who have died am alive again today,
and this is the sun's birthday;this is the birth
day of life and of love and wings:and of the gay
great happening illimitably earth)

how should tasting touching hearing seeing
breathing any—lifted from the no
of all nothing—human merely being
doubt unimaginable You?

(now the ears of my ears awake and
now the eyes of my eyes are opened)

Setting by Peter Dickinson

i thank You God

Peter Dickinson
1965

One afternoon I was lying on my couch,thinking of the usual Nothing,when a sharp cry sung through The Enormous Room

"Il tombe de la neige—Noël! Noël!"

I sat up. The Garde Champêtre was at the nearest window, dancing a little horribly and crying

"Noël! Noël!"

I went to another window and looked out. Sure enough. Snow was falling,gradually and wonderfully falling,silently falling through the thick soundless autumn...It seemed to me supremely beautiful,the snow. There was about it something unspeakably crisp and exquisite,something perfect and minute and gentle and fatal...

...The Enormous Room is filled with a new and beautiful darkness,the darkness of the snow outside,falling and falling and falling with the silent and actual gesture which has touched the soundless country of my mind as a child touches a toy it loves...

Text acknowledged in David Diamond's score
for *The Enormous Room.*

CONDENSED
PROSE

*The very typography of notation of Apollinaire's, E. E.
Cummings', and Ezra Pound's poetry leaves gaps
which let us read through the surface of their verse
back into the intermittent texture of experience.*
        —*Roger Shattuck,* The Banquet Years *(1958)*

The innovations of Cummings' more experimental poetry have
obscured his comparable innovations in the art of prose—inno-
vations that likewise come from shifts in syntax, compression and
extension, a shrewd use of punctuation, and sheer technical
courage. To quote the American poet John Logan again, "The
grammatical inventions (or reintroductions such as the use of
Latin word orders) are designed, some of them, to break up the
usual patterns of response so that the reading *can be* brought
under the control of the poet." Some of these examples of his
prose come from his *Complete Poems* (1991); others are from
texts not currently available in any books.

To Edmund Wilson

Berlin
26 Dezember [1930]

<u>ACHTUNG</u>

Lux is nutn—to uss.

Why for instance:as a boy in a boiled shirt & swallow tails was showing the Nuptial Sweet at Hotel Britannia,Budapest,Hung., he fell flat on the back of his neck at our astonished fruite and— as I faintly endeavored to insert a helpful hand in one prostrate armpit—mercurially arose with the oracular remark(in French) "Par Don". But before that occurence—to be exact,when we boarded the Schnellzug from Munich, Germ.,a wild-eyed official tore into the compartment,placed radio-receivers on our ears,wired the ceiling in a trice,and(presto)we were listening-in-on "Hal Lo Hal Lo Eats Raddy Oh" from the Hung. Broadcasting Co. Headquarters myles & myles away. And don't let nobody tell you there aint magic in Mitl Uropa:why,I asked a ober in Wien for two vermouths please & instead received a cigar! Yes,Berlin is indeed a big place,big and imposturous;but we have sat in the "Wild West" room at Haus Vaterland and looked upon the dunkeles when it was zweimal. Prague,too,contributes her thrills—not to mention trying to explain to a head-czech on a hill that I'd lost the cocher and finally resorting to Ich kam mit ein(?)Mann(?)mit ein(?)Pferd(?)Wo ist er bitte? "The church"he responded laughingly"will be open at 2". And,so it proved. But . . . Keep all this dark from the Doser;as they doubtless are reading about S.Revol.etc.and starvation ad infinatio and besides we're planning to reenter Paris—do I babble on—for New Year's Eve. The trouble with you,Comings,is that you don't no anything—

NOISE

thugs of clumsy mutter shove upward leaving fat
      feet-prints,rumbles poke buzzing thumbs
      in eye of world

stovelike emotion rapidly scrambles toots and
      scurry nibbling screams and sleek
      whistles which sprint ribbons of
      white shriek!   clatters limp,

from svelt blubbering tubes Big dins fuzzily
      lumber rub-bing their eyes

thin very chimney lips wallow gushing cubes
      of unhasty delirium,chunks of
      indolence waddle slowly.

bangs punch.

explosion after

explosion: from black lips sail chrome
      cries extra extra whatisit no?   Yes!
      no! yea: extra wheel! oh hear it
      what no-yes (extra! extra) who, said
      Yea? what! yea! yes.

PEACE Joy's right boot squashes disciplined
      fragilities by slobber of,patient
      timidities undermined skyscrapers,
      Krash;it (explodes in a) plastic Meeow
      —with uncouth snarl of sculptural
      fur through which Claws

      neatly

leap Wall Street wriggles choked with gesturing
        human swill squirms gagged with
        a sprouting filth of faces extra!
        PEACE millions like crabs about a

prosperous penis of bigness the woolworth
        building,slowly waving

factories-stores-houses-burstcrack—people!
        through,doorswindows,Tears a
        vomit of supernatural buttons

PEACE

biffing sky battles huge city which escapes
        niftily through slit-of-sunset
                        Broadway.
        dumb signs ripe

pustules of unhealth.   squEEzed:spatter
        pop-p-ings of mad

colour reveal,

canyons of superb nonsense.   Vistas of
        neatness bunged with a wagging
        humanity poised;In the bathing,

instant   a reek-of electric daintiness PEACE

all night from timetotime the city's accurate
        face peeks from smothering blanket
        of occult pandemonium

PEACE all night!   into dawn-dingy dimness:
        of almost

streets; capers a trickle of mucus
        shapes equals girls men.

it's just like a coffin's
inside when you die,
pretentious and
shiny and
not too wide
                    dear god

there's a portrait
over the door very notable of
the sultan's nose pullable and rosy
flanked by the scrumptious magdalene
of whoisit and madame
something by gainsborough
                            just the playthings
                            for dust   n'est-ce pas

    effendi drifts between
    tables like an old leaf
    between toadstools
he is the cheerfulest of men
    his peaked head smoulders
    like a new turd in April
    his legs are brittle and small
    his feet large and fragile
his queer hands twitter before him,like foolish
    butterflies
he is the most courteous of men

should you remark the walls have been repapered

he will nod
            like buddha
            or answer modestly
i am dying

so let us come in together and
drink coffee covered with froth
half-mud
and not too
sweet?

as usual i did not find him in cafes,the more dissolute atmosphere
of a street superimposing a numbing imperfectness upon such peregri-
nations as twilight spontaneously by inevitable tiredness of flang-
ing shop-girls impersonally affords furnished a soft first clue to
his innumerable whereabouts   violet logic of annihilation demon-
strating from woolworthian pinnacle a capable millennium of faces
meshing with my curiously instant appreciation exposed his hiber-
native contours,
aimiable immensity impeccably extending the courtesy of five o'clock
became the omen of his presence   it was spring by the way in the
soiled canary-cage of largest existence

(when he would extemporise the innovation of muscularity upon the
most crimson assistance of my comforter a click of deciding glory
inflicted to the negative silence that primeval exposure whose elec-
tric solidity remembers some accurately profuse scratchings in a
recently discovered cave,   the carouse of geometrical putrescence
whereto my invariably commendable room has been forever subject his
Earliest word wheeled out on the sunny dump of oblivion)

a tiny dust finely arising at the integration of my soul i coughed

,naturally

gee i like to think of dead it means nearer because deeper firmer
since darker than little round water at one end of the well   it's
too cool to be crooked and it's too firm to be hard but it's sharp
and thick and it loves,   every old thing falls in rosebugs and
jackknives and kittens and pennies they all sit there looking at
each other having the fastest time because they've never met before

dead's more even than how many ways of sitting on your head your
unnatural hair has in the morning

dead's clever too like POF goes the alarm off and the little striker
having the best time tickling away everybody's brain so everybody
just puts out their finger and they stuff the poor thing all full
of fingers

dead has a smile like the nicest man you've never met who maybe winks
at you in a streetcar and you pretend you don't but really you do
see and you are My how glad he winked and hope he'll do it again

or if it talks about you somewhere behind your back it makes your neck
feel pleasant and stoopid   and if dead says may i have this one and
was never introduced you say Yes because you know you want it to dance
with you and it wants to and it can dance and Whocares

dead's fine like hands do you see that water flowerpots in windows but
they live higher in their house than you so that's all you see but you
don't want to

dead's happy like the way underclothes All so differently solemn and
inti and sitting on one string

dead never says my dear,Time for your musiclesson and you like music and
to have somebody play who can but you know you never can and why have to

dead's nice like a dance where you danced simple hours and you take all
your prickly-clothes off and squeeze-into-largeness without one word   and
you lie still as anything   in largeness and this largeness begins to give
you,the dance all over again and you,feel all again all over the way men
you liked made you feel when they touched you(but that's not all)because
largeness tells you so you can feel what you made,men feel when,you touched,
them

dead's sorry like a thistlefluff-thing which goes landing away all by
himself on somebody's roof or something where who-ever-heard-of-growing
and nobody expects you to anyway

dead says come with me he says(andwhyevernot)into the round well and
see the kitten and the penny and the jackknife and the rosebug
                                                              and you
say Sure you say   (like that)   sure i'll come with you you say for i
like kittens i do and jackknives i do and pennies i do and rosebugs i do

my eyes are fond of the east side
as i lie asleep my eyes go into Allen street the dark long cool tunnel
of raving colour,on either side the windows are packed with hardslippery
greens and helplessbaby blues and stic-ky chromes and prettylemons and
virginal pinks and wealthy vermilion and breathless-scarlet,dark colours
like 'cellos keen fiddling colours colours cOOler than harps colours
p r i c k i n g like piccolos thumPing colours like a bangofpiano colours
which,are,the,flowery pluckings of a harpsichord colours of Pure percus-
sion colours-like-trumpets they(writhe they,struggleinweird chords of
humorous,fury heapingandsqueezing tum-bling-scratchingcrowd ingworming
each by screeching Each)on either side the street's DarkcOOllonGBody
windows,are. clenched. fistsoftint.

      TUMTITUMTIDDLE

if sometimes my eyes stay at home
then my mouth will go out into the East side,my mouth goes to the peddlers,
to the peddlers of smooth,fruits of eager colours of the little,huddling
nuts and the bad candies my,mouth loves melons slitted with bright knives,
it stains itself,with currants and cherries it (swallow s bun chesofnew
grapes likeGree n A r e b u b b l e s asc end-ing inthecarts my,mouth
is,fond of tiny plums of tangerines and apples it will,Gorge indistinct
palishflesh of laZilytas tingg OO seberries,it,loves these better than,
cubesandovalsof sweetness but it swallow) s greedily sugaredellipses it
does not disdain picKles,once,it,ate a scarlet pepper and my eyes were
buttoned with pain

      THE BLACK CAT WITH

is there anything my ears love it's
to go into the east Side in a. dark street a hurDygurdY with thequeer
hopping ghosts of children. my,ears know the fuZZy tune that's played
by the Funny hand of the paralyticwhose dod d e rin g partner whEEl
shi min chb yi nch along the whirlingPeaceful furious street people
drop,coppers into,the littletin-cup His wrappedupbody Queerly Has,my,
ears,go into Hassan's place the kanoonchir p ing the bigtwittering
zither-and the mealy,ladies dancing thicklyfoolish,with,the,tam,bou,
rine,s And the violin spitting squeakysongs into the cuspidor-col our-
edRoom and,my ears bend to the little silent handorgan propping the
curve of the tiny motheaten old manwhose Beard rests.onthetopwhose

silly,Hand revolves,perfectly,slowlywith,the handle ofa crankin It
The L's roar tortures-pleasantly myears it is,like the,Jab:of a dark
tool.   With a cleverjeRk in itlike the motionofa Sharp Knife-sN ap-
pingof fadeadf ish' shead Or,the whipping of a blackSnake cu tSudden ly
in 2 that,writhes...A..lit.tleora basket of RipeBlackbeRRies emptied
suddenl (y down the squirming sPine of the)unsuspecting street;
              THE YELLOW EYES AND
—;i Like to
Lie On My Couch at Christopher Street For my stomach goes out into The
east side my sex sitting upright on the stomach like A billiken with
hisknees huggedtogether it,goes out into the rapid hard women and
intotheslow hot women   my Stomach ruBSiTSElf kew-re-ous-ly a mong
Them(among their stomachs andtheir sexes   )stomachsofold pe o pleLike
hideous vegetaBles weazEned with-being-put-too-long in windows and
never sold and couldn't-be-given-away because Who?wanted them,stom-
achslikEDead fishe s s olemnandputrid vast,stomachs bLurting and
cHuckling like uninteresting-landscapes made interesting by earTHQuake
empty stomachsClenche Dtothe beautiful-curveofhunger, cHuBbY stomachs
which have not,known other stomachs and their Sexis a Lone ly,flower
whose secretloveliness hur.ts itse;l.f to no-thing   signifi-cant
stomachs:Who carry-tadpole!s,,stomachs of little,girls smoothanduseless
i,like,best,the,stomachs,of the young (girls silky and lewd)like corn
s l e n derl y tottering in sun-light
              THE
nobody(knows and WhoEver would)?dance lewd dollies pretty and putrid
dollies of-love-and-of-death dollies of perfect life,

dollies of anyway
              VIOLIN

6

dying is fine)but Death

?o
baby
i

wouldn't like

Death if Death
were
good:for

when(instead of stopping to think)you

begin to feel of it,dying
's miraculous
why?be

cause dying is

perfectly natural;perfectly
putting
it mildly lively(but

Death

is strictly
scientific
& artificial &

evil & legal)

we thank thee
god
almighty for dying

(forgive us,o life!the sin of Death

7

at the head of this street a gasping organ is waving moth-eaten
tunes.   a fattish hand turns the crank;the box spouts fairies,out
of it sour gnomes tumble clumsily,the little box is spilling ran-
cid elves upon neat sunlight into the flowerstricken air which is
filthy with agile swarming sonal creatures

—Children,stand with circular frightened faces glaring at the
shabby tiny smiling,man in whose hand the crank goes desperately,
round and round pointing to the queer monkey

(if you toss him a coin he will pick it cleverly from,the air and
stuff it seriously in,his minute pocket)Sometimes he does not
catch a piece of money and then his master will yell at him over
the music and jerk the little string and the monkey will sit,up,
and look at,you with his solemn blinky eyeswhichneversmile and
after he has caught a,penny or three,pennies he will be thrown a
peanut(which he will open skilfully with his,mouth carefully
holding,it,in his little toylike hand)and then he will stiff-ly
throw the shell away with a small bored gesture that makes the
children laugh.

But i don't,   the crank goes round desperate elves and hopeless
gnomes and frantic fairies gush clumsily from the battered box
fattish and mysterious the flowerstricken sunlight is thickening
dizzily is reeling gently the street and the children and the mon-
keyandtheorgan and the man are dancing slowly are tottering up
and down in a trembly mist of atrocious melody....tiniest dead
tunes crawl upon my face my hair is lousy with mutilated singing
microscopic things in my ears scramble faintly tickling putres-
cent atomies,
            and
              i feel the jerk of the little string!the tiny
smiling shabby man is yelling over the music i understand him i
shove my round red hat back on my head i sit up and blink at you
with my solemn eyeswhichneversmile

197

yes,By god.
for i am they are pointing at the queer monkey with a little
oldish doll-like face and hairy arms like an ogre and rubbercolour-
ed hands and feet filled with quick fingers and a remarkable tail
which is allbyitself alive.(and he has a little red coat with i
have a real pocket in it and the round funny hat with a big feather
is tied under myhis chin.)   that climbs and cries and runs and
floats like a toy on the end of a string

8

i was sitting in mcsorley's.   outside it was New York and beauti-
fully snowing.

Inside snug and evil.   the slobbering walls filthily push witless
creases of screaming warmth chuck pillows are noise funnily swallows
swallowing revolvingly pompous a the swallowed mottle with smooth or
a but of rapidly goes gobs the and of flecks of and a chatter sobbings
intersect with which distinct disks of graceful oath,upsoarings the
break on   ceiling-flatness

the Bar.tinking luscious jigs dint of ripe silver with warmlyish
wetflat splurging smells waltz the glush of squirting taps plus slush
of foam knocked off and a faint piddle-of-drops she says I ploc spittle
what the lands thaz me kid in no sir hopping sawdust you kiddo he's a
palping wreaths of badly Yep cigars who jim him why gluey grins topple
together eyes pout gestures stickily point made glints squinting who's
a wink bum-nothing and money fuzzily mouths take big wobbly foot-steps
every goggle cent of it get out ears dribbles soft right old feller
belch the chap hic summore eh chuckles skulch....

and i was sitting in the din thinking drinking the ale,which never
lets you grow old blinking at the low ceiling my being pleasantly was
punctuated by the always retchings of a worthless lamp.

when With a minute terrif   iceffort one dirty squeal of soiling light
yanKing from bushy obscurity a bald greenish foetal head established
It suddenly upon the huge neck around whose unwashed sonorous muscle
the filth of a collar hung gently.

(spattered)by this instant of semiluminous nausea A vast wordless
nondescript genie of trunk trickled firmly in to one exactly-mutilated
ghost of a chair,

a;domeshaped interval of complete plasticity,shoulders,sprouted the
extraordinary arms through an angle of ridiculous velocity commenting
upon an unclean table,and,whose distended immense Both paws slowly
loved a dinted mug

gone Darkness   it was so near to me,i ask of shadow won't you have a
drink?

(the eternal perpetual question)

Inside snugandevil.   i was sitting in mcsorley's   It,did not answer.

outside.(it was New York and beautifully,snowing....

at the ferocious phenomenon of 5 o'clock i find myself gently decompos-
ing in the mouth of New York.   Between its supple financial teeth delir-
iously sprouting from complacent gums,a morsel prettily wanders buoy-
ed on the murderous saliva of industry.   the morsel is i.

Vast cheeks enclose me.

a gigantic uvula with imperceptible gesticulations threatens the tubu-
lar downward blackness occasionally from which detaching itself bumps
clumsily into the throat A meticulous vulgarity:

a sodden fastidious normal explosion;a square murmur,a winsome flatu-
lence—

In the soft midst of the tongue sits the Woolworth building a serene
pastile-shaped insipid kinesis or frail swooping lozenge.   a ruglike
sentience whose papillae expertly drink the docile perpendicular taste
of this squirming cube of undiminished silence,supports while devour-
ing the firm tumult of exquisitely insecure sharp algebraic music.
For the first time in sorting from this vast nonchalant inward walk of
volume the flat minute gallop of careful hugeness i am conjugated by
the sensual mysticism of entire vertical being ,i am skilfully con-
strued by a delicately experimenting colossus whose irrefutable spiral
antics involve me with the soothings of plastic hypnotism   .i am ac-
curately parsed by this gorgeous rush of upward lips....

cleverly

perching on the sudden extremity of one immense tooth myself surveys
safely the complete important profane frantic inconsequential gastro-
nomic mystery of mysteries
                                        ,life

Far below myself the lunging leer of horizontal large distinct ecstasy
wags and.rages   Laughters jostle grins nudge smiles push—.   deep into
the edgeless gloaming gladness hammers incessant putrid spikes of mad-
ness (at

Myself's height these various innocent ferocities are superseded by
the sole prostituted ferocity of silence,it is) still 5 o'clock

I stare only always into the tremendous canyon the

,tremendous canyon always only exhales a climbing dark exact walloping
human noise of digestible millions whose rich slovenly obscene proces-
sion always floats through the thin amorous enormous only lips of the
evening

      And it is 5 o'clock

      in the oblong air,from which a singular ribbon of common sunset
is hanging,

snow speaks slowly

10

THE RAIN IS A HANDSOME ANIMAL

Whereupon i seize a train and suddenly i am in Paris toward night,in Mai.
Along the river trees are letting go scarcely and silently wisps,parcels
of incense,which drop floatingly through a vista of talking moving people;
timidly which caress hats and shoulders,wrists and dresses;which unspeak-
ingly alight upon the laughter of men and children,girls and soldiers.
In twilight these ridiculous and exquisite things descendingly move among
the people,gently and imperishably.   People are not sorry to be alive.
People are not ashamed.   People smile,moving gaily and irrevocably moving
through twilight to The Gingerbread Fair.   I am alive,I go along too,I
slowly go up the vista among the hats and soldiers,among the smiles and
neckties,the kisses and old men,wrists and laughter.   We all together ir-
revocably are moving,are moving slowly and gaily moving.   Intricately the
shoulders of us and our hats timidly are touched by a million absurd hint-
ing things;by wisps and by women and by laughter and by forever:while,
upon our minds,fasten beautifully and close the warm tentacles of evening.

To Edmund Wilson

JOYBARN,nh

eyedz of kaylenz,'30

Gentle Denizens of Thalassaville:

hail!

We,the undersigned,

do hereby proffer our benignities and do very much trust that you survived the Dreadful & Terrible Scene Over The Cut Of Pig;whereof consequences still echo in our surfsmit hearts. Nor shall years(neither time with his scythechariot)ever so much as begin to obliterate—let alone erase—your generosities;to whom ourselves are most fain if all too willing debtors:nevertheless it is our purblind aspiration that you'll give us a whack at evening things up without benefit of underto[w] and allowing for the difference in density between aqua fresh & saline. As for True Row,'tis a mere paddle by comparison with Dune City—but for god's sake watch those O.Jene U.Kneelites and keep 1 weathereye peeled for the bishopy cook John Silver alias Heartofgold. In the name of Harry the Hamlet, Harry the Kemp, and Harry the Rogers Bruce

dingaling

À BAS LES BARRELPIPPILS
VIVE LA VIE
Shantyshantyshantyshantyshantyshantyshanty
hovelhutcabinhouseaboderesidencedemesnemanorcastlepalace-
farmshack

ah,

(wo)

Men.

A thank-you note to Edmund Wilson and his wife from Cummings and his wife after their summer visit to the Wilsons in Provincetown ("Thalassaville") on Cape Cod.

ELLIPTICAL
NARRATIVES

Cummings' tricks of style force us to work with it, as
he has done, experiencing it as plastic and malleable.
We have been given a kitset, not in order to become
carpenters, but to learn the feel of wood.
> —C. K. Stead, "Petal by Petal,"
> London Review of Books *(1933)*

Although Cummings' contribution to the art of fiction is scarcely noticed, I think him among the originators of compressed narrative, where the author focuses a great amount of events and feeling into a few pages—a form that has become more familiar in the later work of Donald Barthelme and Raymond Carver among others since Cummings' death in 1962. This influence alone should refute Hugh Kenner's provocative claim, in *A Homemade World* (1975), of Cummings' unimportance "because Cummings finally altered no verbal environment except his own." Some of these selections were reprinted in his *Complete Poems* (1991).

1

now two old ladies sit peacefully knitting,
and their names are sometimes and always

"i can't understand what life could have seen in him" stitch
-counting always severely remarks;and her sister(suppress-
ing a yawn)counters "o i don't know;death's rather attractive"
—"attractive!why how can you say such a thing?when i think
of my poor dear husband"—"now don't be absurd:what i said was
'rather attractive',my dear;and you know very well that
never was very much more than attractive,never was

stunning"(a crash.   Both jump)"good
heavens!" always exclaims "what
was that?"—"well here comes your daughter"
soothes sometimes;at which

death's pretty young wife enters;wringing her hands,and wailing
"that terrible child!"—"what"(sometimes and always together
cry)"now?"—"my doll:my beautiful doll;the very
first doll you gave me,mother(when i could scarcely
walk)with the eyes that opened and shut(you remember:
don't you,auntie;we called her love)and i've treasured
her all these years,and today i went through a closet
looking for something;and opened a box,and there she
lay:and when he saw her,he begged me to let him
hold her;just once:and i told him 'mankind,be careful;
she's terribly fragile:don't break her,or mother'll be angry' "

and then(except for
the clicking of needles)there was silence

don't get me wrong oblivion
I never loved you kiddo
you that was always sticking around

        spoiling me for everyone else
        telling me how it would make
        you nutty if I didn't let you
        go the distance

and I gave you my breasts to feel
didn't I
     and my mouth to kiss

   O I was too good to you oblivion old kid   that's all
   and when I might have told you

        to go ahead and croak yourselflike
        you was always threatening you was
        going to do
             I didn't
             I said   go on you inter-
             est me
             I let you hang around
             and whimper

   and I've been getting mine
Listen

there's a fellow I love like I never loved anyone else that's six
   foot two tall with a face any girl would die to kiss and a skin
   like a little kitten's
that's asked me to go to Murray's tonight with him and see the cab-
   aret and dance   you know
well
if he asks me to take another I'm going to and if he asks me to take
another after that I'm going to do that and if he puts me into a taxi
and tells the driver to take her easy and steer for the morning I'm
going to let him and if he starts in right away putting it to me in
the cab

I'm not going to whisper
oblivion
do you get me
    not that I'm tired of automats and Childs's and handing out ribbon to
    old ladies that ain't got three teeth and being followed home by pimps
    and stewed guys and sleeping lonely in a whitewashed room three thou-
    sand below Zero   oh no
                          I could stand that
  but it's that I'm O Gawd how tired
                            of seeing the white face of you and
                            feeling the old hands of you and
                            being teased and jollied about you
                            and being prayed and implored and
                            bribed and threatened
to give you my beautiful white body
  kiddo
        that's why

3

"think of it:not so long ago
this was a village"

         "yes;i know"

"of human beings who prayed and sang:
or am i wrong?"

         "no,you're not wrong"

"and worked like hell six days out of seven"
"to die as they lived:in the hope of heaven"

"didn't two roads meet here?"

         "they did;
and over yonder a schoolhouse stood"

"do i remember a girl with blue-
sky eyes and sun-yellow hair?"

         "do you?"

"absolutely"

         "that's very odd,
for i've never forgotten one frecklefaced lad"

"what could have happened to her and him?"
"maybe they waked and called it a dream"

"in this dream were there green and gold
meadows?"

         "through which a lazy brook strolled"

"wonder if clover still smells that way;
up in the mow"

         "full of newmown hay"

"and the shadows and sounds and silences"
"yes,a barn could be a magical place"

"nothing's the same:is it"
      "something still
remains,my friend;and always will"

"namely?"
    "if any woman knows,
one man in a million ought to guess"

"what of the dreams that never die?"
"turn to your left at the end of the sky"

"where are the girls whose breasts begin?"
"under the boys who fish with a pin"

buncha hardboil guys frum duh A.C. fulla
hooch kiddin eachudder bout duh clap an
talkin big how dey could kill
sixereight cops—"I sidesteps im an draws
back huly jeezus"—an—"my
specialty is takin fellers' goils away
frum dem"—"somebody hung uh gun on
Marcus"—"duh Swede rolls down tree flights an Sam
begins boxin im on duh
koib"—you
know
alotta sweet bull like dat

                                           ...suddenly
i feels so lonely fer duh good ole days we
spent in '18 kickin duh guts outa dem
doity frogeaters an humpin duh
swell janes on
duh boollevares an wid tears
streamin down my face i hauls
out uh flask an offers it tuh duh whole gang accrost
duh table—"fellers
have some
on
me"—dey was petrified.

De room swung roun an crawled up into
itself,
an awful big light squoits down my spine like
i was dead er sumpn:next i

knows me(er
somebody is sittin in uh green
field watchin four crows drop into
sunset,playin uh busted harmonica

5

Will i ever forget that precarious moment?

As i was standing on the third rail waiting for the next train to grind me
into lifeless atoms various absurd thoughts slyly crept into my highly sexed
mind.

It seemed to me that i had first of all really made quite a mistake in being
at all born,seeing that i was wifeless and only half awake,cursed with pimples,
correctly dressed,cleanshaven above the nombril,and much to my astonishment much
impressed by having once noticed(as an infantile phenomenon)George Washington al-
most incompletely surrounded by well-drawn icecakes beheld being too strong,in
brief:an American,is you understand that i mean what i say i believe my most
intimate friends would never have gathered.

A collarbutton which had always not nothurt me not much and in the same place.

Why according to tomorrow's paper the proletariat will not rise yesterday.

Inexpressible itchings to be photographed with Lord Rothermere playing with
Lord Rothermere billiards very well by moonlight with Lord Rothermere.

A crocodile eats a native,who in revenge beats it insensible with a banana,
establishing meanwhile a religious cult based on consubstantial intangibility.

Personne ne m'aime et j'ai les mains froides.

His Royal Highness said "peek-a-boo" and thirty tame fleas left the prettily
embroidered howdah immediately.

Thumbprints of an angel named Frederick found on a lightning-rod,Boston,Mass.

such were the not unhurried reflections to which my organ of imperception gave
birth to which i should ordinarily have objected to which,considering the back-
ground,it is hardly surprising if anyone hardly should call exactly extraordin-
ary. We refer,of course,to my position. A bachelor incapable of occupation,he
had long suppressed the desire to suppress the suppressed desire of shall we
say:Idleness,while meaning its opposite? Nothing could be clearer to all con-
cerned than that i am not a policeman.

Meanwhile the tea regressed.

Kipling again H. G. Wells,and Anatole France shook hands again and yet again shook again hands again,the former coachman with a pipewrench of the again latter then opening a box of newly without exaggeration shot with some difficulty sardines. Mr. Wiggin took Wrs. Miggin's harm in is,extinguishing the spittoon by a candle furnished by courtesy of the management on Thursdays,opposite which a church stood perfectly upright but not piano item:a watermelon causes indigestion to William Cullen Longfellow's small negro son,Henry Wadsworth Bryant.

By this time,however,the flight of crows had ceased.   I withdrew my hands from the tennisracket.   All was over.   One brief convulsive octopus,and then our hero folded his umbrella.

It seemed too beautiful.

Let us perhaps excuse me if i repeat himself:these,or nearly these,were the not unpainful thoughts which occupied the subject of our attention;to speak even less objectively,i was horribly scared i would actually fall off the rail before the really train after all arrived.   If i should have made this perfectly clear,it entirely would have been not my fault.

A BOOK
WITHOUT
A TITLE

The danger lies in the neatness of identifications.
—Samuel Beckett, "Dante . . . Bruno . Vico . . Joyce"
(1929)

In contrast to the popular recognition and critical attention Cummings' experiments in verse have provoked, his innovations in prose have been relatively overlooked. Ezra Pound was a notable exception: He placed *Eimi* (1933) alongside James Joyce's *Ulysses* (1922) and Wyndham Lewis' *The Apes of God* (1930) as the greatest prose texts of the modern age because they each reveal the "history of contemporary morals; manner and customs, the REAL history of the ERA." But Cummings' 1929 "A Book without a Title" (also published as *[No Title]* in 1930) depicts another modernist trend, or "history of the ERA": the tradition of narrative experiment exemplified by the work of Gertrude Stein and James Joyce. And yet "A Book" has been consistently dismissed by critics of Cummings as insignificant, or, as Norman Friedman once put it: "There are limits to the fun of pure nonsense." Although it does play within the realm of nonsense, "A Book" is more than an exercise in "fun": It is an extensive provocation of the reader's sense of narrative. It is a text which challenges the way we read.

The compressed and associative narrative can be seen throughout "A Book." The opening sentence of Chapter IV is an example: "Once upon a time,boys and girls,there were two congenital ministers to Belgium,one of whom was insane whereas the other was sixfingered." After the classic fairy tale opening, Cummings immediately throws the reader into a progression of unrelated occurrences which destroys any discernible narrative (we lose sight of the "two congenital ministers" somewhere around the fourth sentence). This leads to the disappointment of narrative expectation the Editor points to: "THIS IS NOT A BOOK!" This rejection of narrative logic is a commentary on how we read "stories."

"A Book" combines one of Cummings' daytime activities—drawing—with his nighttime practice—writing. "A Book" is one of the few of his works bringing together both his art and writing, his pictures and his stories. Books we "know," books we "understand," are made up of stories; and this is, to my mind, the function of the drawings within each chapter: Each drawing represents a story ("THE GARDEN OF EDEN," "THE DEATH OF ABRAHAM LINCOLN," "THE SWAN AND LEDA," "THE DOG IN THE MANGER") which comments upon the way "stories" form and merge and disappear throughout the eight chapters. The "stories" are represented by emblems, tableaus of famous and fabulous scenes from our collective memory of narrative. In this respect, "A Book" plays with the same form of narrative association and compression as *Finnegans Wake;* the story is simple but the means are elaborate, or, as Beckett once wrote of the *Wake:* "Here form *is* content, content *is* form." In this twilight of prose and drawings, the function of narrative is highlighted and then erased.

The entire "book" is only thirty-one pages long. Chapter 1 is reprinted here.

—John Rocco

1. *THE GARDEN OF EDEN*
. . . before the dawn of history . . .

CHAPTER I

The king took off his hat and looked at it. Instantly an immense crowd gathered. The news spread like wildfire. From a dozen leading dailies,reporters and cameramen came rushing to the scene pellmell in highpowered monoplanes. Hundreds of reserves,responding without hesitation to a riotcall,displayed with amazing promptness quite unparalleled inability to control the everincreasing multitude,but not before any number of unavoidable accidents had informally occurred. A G.A.R. veteran with aluminum legs,for example,was trampled and the nonartificial portions of his heroic anatomy reduced to pulp. Twin anarchists(one of whom was watering chrysanthemums five miles away and the other of whom was fast asleep in a delicatessen)were immediately arrested,devitalized,and jailed, on the charge of habeas corpus with premeditated arson. A dog, stepped on,bit in the neck a beautiful highstrung woman who had for some time suffered from insomnia and who—far too enraged to realize,except in a very general way,the source of the pain—instantly struck a child of four,knocking its front teeth out. Another woman,profiting by the general excitement, fainted and with a hideous shriek fell through a plateglass window. On the outskirts of the throng,several octogenarians succumbed to hearttrouble with grave external complications. A motorcycle ran over an idiot. A stonedeaf nightwatchman's left eye was exterminated by the point of a missing spectator's parasol. Sinking seven storeys from a nearby officebuilding,James Anderson(coloured)landed in the midst of the crowd absolutely unhurt,killing eleven persons including the ambassador to Uruguay. At this truly unfortunate occurrence,one of the most prominent businessmen of the city,William K. Vanderdecker,a member of the Harvard,Yale,and Racquet Clubs,swallowed a cigar and died instantly;leaving to fifty plainclothesmen the somewhat difficult task of transporting his universally lamented remains three and one-third miles to a waiting ambulance where they were given first aid,creating an almost unmentionable disturbance during which everybody lost caste and the

218

Rev. Donald X. Wilkins received internal injuries resulting in his becoming mentally deficient and attempting to undress on the spot. Needless to say,the holy man was prevented by wrathful bystanders from carrying out his ignominious plan,and fell insensible to the sidewalk. Calm had scarcely been restored,when a petty officer from the battleship Idaho was seized with delirium tremens. In still another part of the mob,a hydrant exploded without warning,causing no casualties. Olaf Yansen,a plumber,and a floorwalker,Isidor Goldstein,becoming mutually infuriated owing to some probably imaginary difference of opinion,resorted to a spontaneous display of physical culture,in the course of which the former(who,according to several witnesses,was getting the worst of it,in spite of his indubitably superior size)hit the latter with a brick and vanished. Mr. Goldstein is doing well. While playing with a box of peppermints which his parents,Mr. and Mrs. Aloysius Fitzroy of 96 Hoover Ave. Flatbush,had given their little son Frank Jr. to keep him quiet,the infant(in some unaccountable manner)set fire to forty-one persons,of whom thirty-nine were burned to ashes. A Chinese,Mi Wong,who exercises the profession of laundryman at 686 868th Street and Signor Alhambra,a millionaire Brazilian coffeeplanter who refused to be interviewed and is stopping at the Ritz,are the survivors. Havoc resulted when one of the betterliked members of the young married set, whose identity the authorities refused to divulge,kissed Tony Crack,iceman,on the spur of the moment,receiving concussion of the brain with black eyes. In the front rank of onlookers,a daughter of the people became so excited by His Majesty's spectacular act that before you could say Jack Robinson she emitted triplets.

But such trivial catastrophes were rapidly eclipsed by a disaster of really portentous significance. No sooner had the stockexchange learned what the king had done,than an unprecedented panic started;and the usually stable Lithuanian kopec zoomed in seventeen minutes from nine hundred decimal point three to decimal point six zeros eight seven four five,wiping out at one fell swoop the solidlyfounded fortunes of no less than two thousand two hundred and two pillars of society,and exerting an overpowering influence for evil on wheat and sugar,not to mention the national industry(kerosene)—all three of which tumbled about in a frightful manner. The president of the India Rubber Trust Co.,bareheaded and with his false hair streaming in the wind,tore out of the Soldiers' and Sailors' Savings Bank, carrying in one hand a pet raccoon belonging to the president of the latter institution,Philip B. Sears,and in the other a telephone which the former had(in the frenzy of the moment)forgotten to replace on his distinguished confrère's desk. A hookandladder,driven by Abraham Abrahams at a speed of $(a+b)^{a+b}$ miles an hour,passed over the magnate longitudinally as he crossed Dollar Row and left a rapidly expiring corpse automatically haranguing an imaginary board of directors;and whose last words—spoken into the(oddly enough)unbroken mouthpiece of the instrument only to be overheard by Archibald Hammond,a swillman—were:"Let us then if you please." So unnerved was the Jehu of the Clipton St. firestation by this totally unexpected demise that,without pausing to consider the possible damage to life and limb involved in a purely arbitrary deviation from the none-too-ample throughfare,he declined the very next corner in favour of driving straight though the city's largest skyscraper;whose one hundred and thirteen storeys— after tottering horribly for a minute and a half—reeled and thundered earthward with the velocity of light,exterminating every vestige of humanity and architecture within a radius of eighteen miles. This paralysing cataclysm was immediately followed by a colossal conflagration of stupendous proportions whose prodigiously enormous flames,greedily winding themselves around the few remaining outhouses,roasted by myriads the inhabitants thereof;while generating a heat so terrific as to evaporate the largest river of the kingdom—which,completely disappearing in less than eleven seconds,revealed a giltedged submarine of the UR type,containing(among other things)the entire royal family(including the king,who still held his hat in his hand)in the act of escaping,disguised as cheeses.

FILM
SCENARIO

*An idea of the theater has been lost. And as long as
the theater limits itself to showing us intimate scenes
from the lives of a few puppets, transforming the pub-
lic into Peeping Toms, it is no wonder the elite aban-
don it and the great public looks to the movies, the
music hall, or the circuses for violent satisfactions,
whose intentions do not deceive them.*
—Antonin Artaud, The Theatre and Its Double *(1938)*

In "The New Art," his commencement speech given at Harvard
in 1915, Cummings discussed the progress of four types of art:
painting, sculpture, music, and literature. But Cummings became
aware of even "newer" forms of art as his interest in art branched
out into an interest into popular culture. This is expressed in the
wide variety of topics he wrote about in *Vanity Fair* during the
'20s. His subjects ranged from "American Sex magazines" to Jean
Cocteau, from burlesque to the dynamics of viewing animals in
a zoo, from an analysis of the circus to a description of the aes-
thetics of Coney Island. Cummings brings to his description of
something like Coney Island the same kind of wide-eyed exuber-
ance and incisive cultural criticism that Tom Wolfe would bring
to his visit to Las Vegas years later. And unlike the American High
Modernist poets who only used aspects of popular American cul-
ture as contrasting or humorous elements in their work—Pound's
"incorporation" of black speech into *The Pisan Cantos,* for exam-

221

ple—Cummings was consistently provoked by and concerned with popular culture in all its forms. "A Pair of Jacks" is his foray into the popular form of film—a foray that displays his knowledge of the medium as well as his concern with its tropes.

"A Pair of Jacks" is a parody (it was first published under the title " 'Vanity Fair's Prize Movie scenario' by one C. E. Niltse, 'A Master of Screen Continuity' " in 1925); and in it Cummings illustrates aspects of the medium—montage, timing, points of view—with aspects of the popular genres—melodrama, comedy—in a scenario that seems to flout its chances of ever being produced. "A Pair of Jacks" was written in the late silent era of Hollywood films and everything in it—from its array of odd characters, its collection of exotic scenes, its rapid editing, its titles·— reflects the concerns of American popular film. As a reader of film, Cummings produced a scenario that tells us a great deal about the movies while it challenges the very basis of our conception of them.

—John Rocco

A PAIR OF JACKS

FADE IN TITLE: *In the sleepy province of Zinacantepec, North-ern China, not far from the picturesque valley of the Tlaxcala, and near the Apetatian Mountains, lounges the drowsy village of Xochilhuehuetlan.*

SCENE 1. Exterior Countryside. FADE IN, on a LONG SHOT of a lovely African landscape, the foothills hazy in the background, and a one-horned Indian rhinoceros nursing its young in the foreground.

TITLE: *Mother love is mother love, no matter where it occurs.*

SCENE 2. Exterior Town. A FULL SHOT of the otzolote pee, or mayor, of Xochilhuehuetlan. He is a young woman, with a centripetal red beard. He is between ninety-eight and ninety-nine years old, a type of the typical centrifugal hermaphrodite of the country. His face is large and small, he has the muscular fragility of a sixteen year old baby; there is about him the inherent inebriety of a recently cauterized factotum. He is deep, but also he is round—the mendacity and the propinquity of the Celt lie side by side in his down-right Iberian make-up. He is sucking a snake bite in his ear, and waiting for death.

TITLE: *Tamanlipas Guerrero, whose fingers are five in number, was not afraid to die.*

Back for a glimpse of the official as he sucks his snake bite. There is a flicker of scorn for the snake's treachery on his face.

SCENE 3. Exterior Deck. FADE IN on a SEMICLOSEUP of a young girl. She is a mature, manly Negress, with a jade nose-ring, protruding lips, and a wooden leg, dressed in a middy blouse and hip rubberboots over which is thrown carelessly a pair of silk stockings. She is standing wildly by a ventilator and gazing throbbingly over the entire ship, on which everyone else is seasick, as vast breakers dash fiercely from time to time over the entire ship, and as a baby rolls at intervals into the scuppers she stoops and gives the little one a kiss.

TITLE: *In the meantime, Elizabeth Bilge, the girl who held Jack Water's esteem, is peacefully cruising homeward.*

SCENE 4. Interior Home. IRIS IN on a New England Homestead, in the foreground Granny is knitting as a mischievous kitten is playing with the yarn, while Mother reads aloud to father, Kitty and Tom, who are both obviously overinterested in each other. In the background, a glimpse of snowcovered Mount Chocorua, named after an old Indian chief and 3,540 feet above sea level.

TITLE: *But the spirit of the hour and the old traditions are not the same like they was once when Mother was a girl.*

SCENE 5. MEDIUM SHOT of a perfectly terrible storm at sea. Even the captain does not know what to do. It is terrible. They will all be drowned. Terrible waves are dashing over the poor ship which is sometimes underneath the top of the water, smashing all the lifeboats. With a terrible crash the unhappy ship strikes a submerged cliff.

TITLE: *Jack Clinton, gentleman garter salesman, had a way with him, and with the ladies.*

SCENE 6. Interior Cabin. CLOSEUP of Jack. The water is pouring in, but he is awake in his pyjamas. The ill-starred ship is sinking. He unwinds the alarm clock with a smile. The bed with everything on it collapses without warning, as, without meaning to, he picks up a telephone. CUT TO

SCENE 7. The Bottom of the Sea, 9:55 A.M. Interior Cabin. Exterior Town. A shot of a submarine cable winding and unwinding along the valleys of the mountainous sea bottom. Simultaneously each side of this shot recedes toward the middle, discovering, on the left, Jack at his telephone, on the right, Tamanlipas at his telephone, until the cable disappears wholly and Jack and Tamanlipas confront each other in one scene. Dissolve out the telephone. From this point on the two men play their scene as if back to back against a neutral foreground.

SCENE 8. Interior Cabin. Water pours in deluging Jack who, smiling, hangs up the phone. As he does so—

SCENE 9. The Bottom of the Sea, 9:56 A.M. Interior Cabin. Exterior Town. The scene breaks in the middle, going back on each side, cutting off the shots of Jack and Tamanlipas, discovering the submarine cable along the bottom of the sea once more.

SCENE 10. Exterior Town. Tamanlipas Guerrero, nursing his snake bite, puts down the telephone to die.

TITLE: *And the sun's last rays reflected the passing of a good Indian.*

SCENE 11. Exterior Deck. Shot of Jack Clinton with Elizabeth Bilge in his arms lowering himself from the rail to the open sea on a pair of Boston garters which he has tied to the rail with his free hand as waves pour all over the entire ship and everyone is very sick.

SCENE 12. Exterior Home. MEDIUM SHOT of Grandma standing gracefully on a piano stool in the middle of the front yard. Above her head is the limb of an apple tree in full bloom. About six inches from the old lady's nose is a nest into which she is looking. as the excited mother bird beats her wings frantically.

SPOKEN TITLE: *"Don't worry, birdie, Granny won't hurt your babies!"*

SCENE 13. The Middle of the Ocean. IRIS IN on Jack Waters standing in his twelve-cylinder Ford sedan, as he spies the scene at one glance of the naked eye. He is a clean-cut, well-dressed, happy-go-lucky will-o'-the-wisp with a bad record at Yale to the credit of his twenty-three years as a rich man's pampered and only son, holding under one muscular arm a tennis racquet. There is something about him which courts dangers of every sort. He laughs and says:

SPOKEN TITLE: *"Give me the binoculars, Captain, it looks like a cane rush!"*

SCENE 14. Interior Heaven. LONG SHOT of the gates of Heaven: God, angels, cherubim, seraphim, etc. The soul of Tamanlipas Guerrero is walking toward a little house. It is dressed in a crêpe-de-Chine nightie, a straw hat with a fraternity band, and is smoking a pipe. God turns to Michael for information about the unknown visitor. Michael says it is a good Indian. God speaks:

SPOKEN TITLE: *"Bid him welcome, then, in the name of all that is good."*

SCENE 15. Exterior Deck. Jack Clinton's eyes flash black lightning as, with an oath, he falls into the sea with Elizabeth Bilge in his arms as the garters break, and is drowned.

225

TITLE: *But for once in his life, the clever salesman of a next-to-indispensable commodity found his match in a watery grave.*

SCENE 16. Interior Nest. CLOSEUP of five eggs as one of them begins to hatch.

TITLE: *"Peep, peep."*

Back for a look at Granny's wrinkled smiling face as it regards the hatching progeny. Over the tired eyes comes an expression of broad laughter.

SCENE 17. The Middle of the Ocean. FADE IN on a CLOSEUP of Captain Black of the Ford Sedan, as he hands Jack Waters the binoculars. He is rugged, rough, robust, uncouth, short-spoken, good-hearted, horny-handed, two-fisted, ten-toed specimen of master mariner with a father complex.

SPOKEN TITLE: *"Here they be, God bless you, Mister Jack!"*

SCENE 18. Exterior Deck. MEDIUM SHOT of Elizabeth Bilge who struggles with the waves, supported by her wooden leg. About to go down for the first time, she shouts:

SPOKEN TITLE: *"Save me!"*

SCENE 19. Interior Heaven. CLOSEUP of the soul of Tamanlipas Guerrero. Its eyes are fixed on the little house, at a point just over the door, where there is a sign in large letters: Caballeros. Tamanlipas Guerrero's soul does not read or write. What a terrible predicament! Just then along comes Michael. The soul hails him and asks him something. Michael nods and smiles. The soul starts to hurry off in the direction of the house, when Michael lays a detaining hand on its arm, saying:

SPOKEN TITLE: *"I am instructed to bid you welcome, spirit. You are now in Heaven."*

SCENE 20. The Middle of the Ocean. LONG SHOT of Jack Waters looking through the binoculars. As he sees something, the glasses fall from his nerveless hands. At the same moment he falls himself but is caught by Captain Black, who works over him for some time with a stomach pump, until the young man's eyes open. Gazing indistinctly at the Captain, the youth of whom Elizabeth Bilge held the esteem murmurs:

SPOKEN TITLE: *"Full speed ahead!"*

SCENE 21. Exterior Home. MEDIUM SHOT of Granny as

she gracefully descends from the piano stool. (Hold long enough for human interest.) Shutting her umbrella she enters the house, whereupon it stops raining and the sun comes out.

SCENE 22. Cross section of the Ocean. CLOSEUP of the descending binoculars, which have fallen overboard, as they start toward the bottom of the sea. Some local colour: a frightened fish or two, for instance.

(Note: if we could rent an octopus, or something, it would be good here.)

TITLE: *Meanwhile, giving free rein to their intrinsic curiosity, a pair of lenses spontaneously traverse the dim domain of Neptune.*

SCENE 23. Interior Heaven. LONG SHOT of the soul of Tamanlipas Guerrero, as it exits from the little house registering blissful contentment. It says to Michael, touchingly:

SPOKEN TITLE: *"Heaven is right."*

SCENE 24. IRIS IN on a YIDDISH PICNIC IN THE CATSKILLS. About a fire of driftwood made by girl scouts are seated thousands and thousands of Hebrew maidens, their faces are chewing gum and smileless. A slight dark slip of a feminine thing in the foreground investigates a recently-opened can of sardines.

TITLE: *Lizzie Finklestein, who plays the violin beautifully.*

SCENE 25. The Bottom of the Sea. MEDIUM SHOT of binoculars as they come to rest on the volcano-strewn sea bottom. (Perhaps a whale passes, pursued by another whale, or almost anything to give local colour.)

SCENE 26. Interior Home. The old mother falls down a flight of stairs and breaks both her legs simultaneously as Jack Waters, torn between his devotion to his parent and his love for Elizabeth Bilge, does not hesitate a moment, then turns the rudder of the Ford sedan backward and is soon carrying the delighted old lady in his aeroplane to Captain Black's half-brother's expensive sanatorium, while Lizzie Finklestein plays her instrument so lovely, until all the picknickers fall one by one asleep, then gets into a breeches buoy and in that terrible predicament rescues Jack Clinton who was not drowned as we all thought, but at this moment a birth certificate is discovered proving that the ghost of Tamanlipas Guerrero is a fourth cousin to Dr.

Marie Stopen, whereupon a lawn party is given for no reason whatever by Mrs. Harry Payne Whitney and everyone dances to general hilarity, as

SCENE 27. Exterior Moon Night. CLOSEUP of a cloud. It nears the moon. It passes over the moon. The moon disappears. The cloud moves on. The moon reappears. A tree appears in front of the moon. A nest appears upon a limb. In the nest are five eggs. Thunder and lightning. All hatch suddenly.

TITLE: *"Poems are made by fools like me, only God can make a tree."*

VERY SLOW FADE-OUT

TRANSLATION

*My theory of techique, if I have one, is very far from
original; nor is it complicated. I can express it in fif-
teen words, by quoting the Eternal Question And
Immortal Answer of burlesk, vis. "Would you hit a
woman with a child? No, I'd hit her with a brick."
Like the burlesk comedian, I am abnormally fond of
that precision which creates movement.*
        —E. E. Cummings, foreword to Is 5 *(1926)*

Cummings was also an occasional translator from the
Romance languages. The *Complete Poems* (1991) reprints his
translations from the Latin poet Horace, while the English libretto
of Igor Stravinsky's oratorio *Oedipus Rex* (1927) represents Cum-
mings' translation of a text that Jean Cocteau originally wrote in
both French *and* Latin. Here are the opening and the closing of
Cummings' contemporaneous translation of Louis Aragon's long
poem, *Front Rouge* (1931), which we print along with the origi-
nal, to demonstrate not only the translator's fluency but also his
accuracy.

Louis Aragon

FRONT ROUGE

Une douceur pour mon chien
Un doigt de champagne Bien Madame
Nous sommes chez Maxim's l'an mille
Neuf cent trente
On met des tapis sous les bouteilles
Pour que leur cul d'aristocrate
ne se heurte pas aux difficultés de la vie
des tapis pour cacher la terre
des tapis pour éteindre
le bruit de la semelle des chaussures des garcons
Les boissons se prennent avec des pailles
qu'on tire d'un petit habit de précaution
Délicatesse
Il y a des fume-cigarettes entre la cigarette et l'homme
des silencieux aux voitures
des escaliers de service pour ceux
qui portent les paquets
et du papier de soie autour des paquets
et du papier autour du papier de soie
du papier tant qu'on veut cela ne coûte
rien le papier ni le papier de soie ni les pailles
ni le champagne ou si peu
ni le cendrier réclame ni le buvard
réclame ni le calendrier
réclame ni les lumières
réclame ni les images sur les murs
réclame ni les fourrures sur Madame
réclame réclame les cure-dents
réclame l'éventail et réclame le vent
rien ne coûte rien et pour rien
des serviteurs vivants vous tendent dans la rue des prospectus
Prenez c'est gratis
le prospectus et la main qui le tend
Ne fermez pas la porte

1

THE RED FRONT

A gentleness for my dog
A finger of Champagne Very well Madame
We are at Maxim's A.D. one thousand
nine hundred thirty
Carpets have been put under the bottles
so that their aristocratic arses
may not collide with life's difficulties
there are carpets to hide the earth
there are carpets to extinguish
the noise of the soles of the waiters' shoes
Drinks are sipped through straws
which you pull out of a little safety-dress
Delicacy
There are cigaretteholders between cigarette and man
there are silent people at the cars
there are service-stairs for those
who carry packages
and there's tissue paper around the packages
and there's paper around the tissue paper
there's all the paper you want that doesn't cost
anything paper nor tissue paper nor straws
nor champagne or so little
nor the advertisement-ashtray, nor the
advertisement-blotter nor the
advertisement-calendar nor the
advertisement-lights nor the
advertisement-pictures on the walls nor the
advertisement-furs on Madame the
advertisement-toothpicks the advertisement-fan and the advertisement wind
nothing costs anything and for nothing
real live servitors, tender you prospectuses in the street
Take it, it's free
the prospectus and the hand which tenders it
Don't close the door

le Blount s'en chargera Tendresse
Jusqu'aux escaliers qui savent monter seuls
dans les grands magasins
Les journées sont de feutre
les hommes de brouillard Monde ouaté
sans heurt
Vous n'êtes pas fous Des haricots Mon chien
n'a pas encore eu la maladie

O pendulettes pendulettes
avez-vous assex fait rêver les fiancés sur les grands boulevards
et le lit Louis XVI avec un an de crédit
Dans les cimetières les gens de ce pays si bien huilé
se tiennent avec la décence du marbre
leurs petites maisons ressemblent
à des dessus de cheminée

Combien coûtent les chrysanthèmes cette année

Fleurs aux morts fleurs aux grandes artistes
L'argent se dépense aussi pour l'idéal
Et puis les bonnes œuvres font traîner des robes noires
dans des escaliers je ne vous dis que ca
La princesse est vraiment trop bonne
Pour la reconnaissance qu'on vous en a
A peine s'ils vous remercient
C'est l'exemple des bolchéviques
Malheureuse Russie
L'U. R. S. S.
L'U. R. S. S. ou comme ils disent S. S. S. R.
S. S. comment est-ce S. S.
S. S. R. S. S. R. S. S. S. R. oh ma chère
Pensez donc S. S. S. R.
Vous avez vu
les grèves du Nord
Je connais Berck et Paris-plage
Mais non les grèves SSSR
SSSR SSSR SSSR

232

the Blount will take care of that Tenderness
Up to the very stairs which know how to ascend by themselves
in the department stores
Days are made of felt
Men are made of fog The world is padded
without collision
You aren't crazy Some beans My dog
hasn't been sick yet

O little clocks little clocks
have you given enough dreams to the lovers on the great boulevards
and the Louis XVI bed with a year's credit
In the cemeteries the people of this so-well-oiled country
hold themselves with the decency of the marble
Their little houses resemble
chimneypots

How much are chrysanthemums this year

Flowers for the dead flowers for the great artistes
Money is also spent for ideals
And besides good deeds wear long black trailing gowns
on the stairs I only tell you that
The princess is really too kind
for the gratitude which is owed you
Scarcely if they thank you
It's the bolsheviks' example
Unhappy Russia
The URSS
The URSS or as they say SSSR
SS how is it SS
SSR SSR SSR oh my dear
just think SSSR
You have seen
the strikes in the North
I know Berck and Paris-plage
But not the strikes in the SSSR
SSSR SSSR SSSR

L'intervention devait débuter par l'entrée en scène de la Roumanie sous le prétexte, par exemple, d'un incident de frontière, entraînant la déclaration officielle de la guerre par la Pologne, et la solidarisation des Etats limitrophes. A cette intervention se seraient jointes les troupes de Wrangle qui auraient traversé la Roumanie...A leur retour de la conférence énergétique de Londres, se rendant en U. R. S. S. par Paris, Ramzine et Leritchev ont organisé la liaison avec le Torgprom par l'intermédiaire de Riabouchinski qui entretenait des rapports avec le Gouvernement français en la personne de Loucheur...Dans l'organisation de l'intervention le rôle directeur appartient à la France qui en a conduit la préparation avec l'aide active du Gouvernement anglais...

Les chiens les chiens les chiens conspirent
et comme le tréponème pâle échappe au microscope
Poincaré se flatte d'être un virus filtrant
La race des danseurs de poignards des maquereaux tzaristes
les grands ducs mannequins des casinos qu'on lance
Les délateurs à 25 francs la lettre
la grande pourriture de l'émigration
lentement dans le bidet français se cristallise
La morve polonaise et la bave roumaine
la vomissure du monde entier
s'amassent à tous les horizons du pays où se construit le socialisme
et les têtards se réjouissent
se voient déjà crapauds
décorés
députés qui sait ministres
Eaux sales suspendez votre écume
Eaux sales vous n'êtes pas le déluge
Eaux sales vous retomberez dans le bourbier occidental
Eaux sales vous ne couvrirez pas les plaines où pousse le blé pur du devenir
Eaux sales Eaux sales vous ne dissoudrez pas l'oseille de l'avenir
Vous ne souillerez pas les marches de la collectivisation
Vous mourrez au seuil brûlant de la dialectique
de la dialectique aux cent tours porteuses de flammes écarlates
aux cent mille tours qui crachent le feu de mille et mille canons
Il faut que l'univers entende

Intervention should begin with the appearance of Rumania on the scene, on the pretext, for instance, of some trouble on the frontier involving an official declaration of war by Poland and the joining together of the troops of Wrangel which would have traversed Rumania...On their return from the energetic conference of London, entering the URSS from Paris, Ramzine and Leritchev have organized communication with the Torgprom through the intermediary of Riabouchinski, who was keeping up relations with the French government personified by Loucheur...In the organization of the intervention the chief role belongs to France which has prepared it with the active aid of the English government...

The dogs the dogs the dogs are conspiring
and as the pale tréponème escapes the microscope
Poincaré flatters himself that he's a filtering poison
The race of the daggerdancers of the tzarist pimps
the dummy grand-dukes of the casinos which we lance
the informers who charge 25 francs a letter
the huge rottenness of emigration
slowly crystallizes in the French bidet
The Polish snot and the Rumanian drivel
the puke of the whole world
are massed on the horizons of the country where socialism builds itself
and the tadpoles rejoice
see themselves already as frogs
with decorations
deputies who knows ministers
Foul waters suspend your foam
Foul waters you are not the deluge
Foul waters you will fall again in the occidental slough
Foul waters you will not cover the plains where sprouts the pure wheat of the
Foul waters Foul waters you will not dissolve the sorrel of the future   [future
You will not soil the steps of collectivization
You will die at the burning threshold of a dialectic
of a dialectic with a hundred turnings which carry scarlet flames
with a hundred thousand turnings which spit the fire of thousands and
The universe must hear   [thousands of canons

une voix hurler la gloire de la dialectique matérialiste
qui marche sur ses pieds sur ses millions de pieds
chaussés de bottes militaires
sur ses pieds magnifiques comme la violence
tendant sa multitude de bras armés
vers l'image du Communisme vainqueur
Gloire à la dialectique matérialiste
et gloire à son incarnation
l'armée
Rouge
Gloire à
l'armée
Rouge
Une étoile est née de la terre
Une étoile aujourd'hui mène vers une bûche de feu
les soldats de Boudenny
En marche soldats de Boudenny
Vous êtes la conscience en armes du Prolétariat
Vous savez en portant la mort
à quelle vie admirable vous faites une route
Chacun de vos corps est un diamant qui tombe
Chacun de vos vers un feu qui purifie
L'éclair de vos fusils fait reculer l'ordure
France en tête
N'épargnez rien soldats de Boudenny
Chacun de vos cris porte au loin l'Haleine embrasée
de la Révolution Universelle
Chacune de nos respirations propage
Marx et Lénine dans le ciel
Vous êtes rouges comme l'aurore
rouges comme la colére
rouges comme le sang
Vous vengez Babeuf et Liebknecht
Prolétaires de tous les pays unissez-vous
Voix Appelez-les préparez leur la
voie à ces libérateurs qui joindront aux vôtres
leurs armes Prolétaires de tous les pays
Voici la catastrophe apprivoisée

236

a voice yelling the glory of materialistic dialectic
marching on its feet on its millions of feet
booted with army boots
on feet magnificent like violence
outstretching its multitudinous warrior-arms
toward the image of triumphant Communism
Hail to materialistic dialectic
and hail to its incarnation
the Red
army
Hail to
the Red
army
A star is born on earth
A star today leads toward a fiery breach
the soldiers of Budenny
March on soldiers of Budenny
You are the armed conscience of the Proletariat
You know while you carry death
to what admirable life you are making a road
Each of your blows is a diamond which falls
Each of your steps a fire which purifies
The lightning of your guns makes ordure recoil
France at the head
Spare nothing soldiers of Budenny
Each of your cries carries afar the firefilled Breath
of Universal Revolution
Each of your breathings begets
Marx and Lenin in the sky
You are red like the dawn
red like anger
red like blood
You avenge Babeuf and Liebknecht
Proletarians of all countries unite your
Voices Call them prepare for them the
way to those liberators who shall join with yours
their weapons Proletarians of all countries
Behold the tamed catastrophy

Voici docile enfin la bondissante panthère
L'Histoire menée en laisse par la troisième Internationale
le train rouge s'ébranle et rien ne l'arrêtera
U R
S S
U R
S S
U R
S S
Il n'y a personne qui reste en arrière
agitant des mouchoirs Tout le monde est en marche
U R
S S
U R
S S
Inconscients oppositionnels
Il n'y a pas de frein sur la machine
Hurle écrasé mais le vent chante
U R
SS SS
SR UR
SS SSSR
Debout les damnés de la terre
S R
S S
S R
S S
Le passé meurt l'instant embraye
SSSR SSSR
les roues s'élancent le rail chauffe SSSR
Le train s'emballe vers demain
SSSR toujours plus vite SSSR
En quatre ans le plan quinquennal
SSSR à bas l'exploitation de l'homme par l'homme
SSSR à bas l'ancien servage à bas le capital
à bas l'impérialisme à bas
SSSR SSSR SSSR

Behold docile at last the bounding panther
History led on leash by the third International
The red train starts and nothing shall stop it
UR
SS
UR
SS
UR
SS
No one remains behind
waving handkerchiefs Everyone is going
UR
SS
UR
SS
Unconscious opposers
There are no brakes on the engine
Howl crushed but the wind sings
UR
SS SS
SS UR
SS SSSR
Up you damned of earth
SS
SR
SS
SR
The past dies the moment is thrown into gear
SSSR SSSR
the roads spring the rail warms SSSR
the train plunges toward tomorrow
SSSR ever faster SSSR
In four years the fiveyearplan
SSSR down with the exploiting of man by man
SSSR down with the old bondage down with capital
down with imperialism down with it!
SSSR SSSR SSSR

Ce qui grandit comme un cri dans les montagnes
Quand l'aigle frappé relâche soudainement ses serres
SSSR SSSR SSSR
C'est le chant de l'homme et son rire
C'est le train de l'étoile rouge
qui brûle les gares les signaux les airs
SSSR octobre octobre c'est l'express
octobre à travers l'univers SS
SR SSSR SSSR
SSSR SSSR

That which swells like a cry in the mountains
When the stricken eagle suddenly lets go with its talons
SSSR SSSR SSSR
It's the song of man and his laughter
It's the train of the red star
which burns the stations the signals the skies
SSSR October October it's the express
October across the universe SS
SR SSSR SSSR
SSSR SSSR

ARTS
CRITICISM

Why should the excellences of American theater be so radically unlike the best of Europe? Let me suggest that the causes lie partially in our perceptibly different attitudes toward theater; for the fact that we spell the word differently—er, rather than re—symbolically indicates larger discrepancies. When Americans, both highbrow and low, gather together, they feel more comfortable in informal atmospheres—in sports arenas and at parties. "Legitimate theater" they regard as a forbidding temple, to be entered only on special (and expensive) occasions.
—Richard Kostelanetz, "The American Tradition of Theater" (1972)

In what way does Krazy Kat's vocabulary resemble Doctor Johnson's?
—Edmund Wilson, "Gilbert Seldes and the Popular Arts" (1924)

In his Harvard commencement address in 1915, Cummings displayed his familiarity with new developments in all the arts—not only literature but music and visual art. It follows that many of his early critical essays, most of which were published before he turned thirty-five, were concerned not only with poetry but with sculpture, graphics, film, various kinds of nonliterary performance, and even comic strips. Indeed, "The New Art" (1915) represents an American antecedent to Guillaume Apollinaire's classic "The New Spirit and the Poets" (1917) as the epitome of a young man's perspicacious understandings. In retrospect we can also say that Cummings was the first theater critic to recognize what we now call performance art and to praise it over drama, the first to find theatrical value in the playgrounds of Coney Island, and the first to understand animated film. My colleague John Rocco thinks that in this respect Cummings became an avatar of what is now called Cultural Studies. While the first essay is reprinted in its entirety, the others are abridged. At the end of this section are some of the 1925 parodies of criticism that stylistically presage, especially in their quick shifts and pervasively irreverent tone, the writings of S. J. Perelman (1904–79).

THE NEW ART

The New Art has many branches—painting, sculpture, architecture, the stage, literature, and music. In each of these there is a clearly discernible evolution from models; in none is there any trace of that abnormality, or incoherence, which the casual critic is fond of making the subject of tirades against the new order.

It is my purpose to sketch briefly the parallel developments of the New Art in painting, sculpture, music, and literature.

I.

Anyone who takes Art seriously, who understands the development of technique in the last half century, accepts Cezanne and Matisse as he accepts Manet and Monet. But this brings us to the turning point where contemporary criticism becomes, for the most part, rampant abuse, and where prejudice utters its storm of condemnation. I refer to that peculiar phase of modern art called indiscriminately, "Cubism," and "Futurism."

The name Cubism, properly applied, relates to the work of a small group of ultramodern painters and sculptors who use design to express their personal reaction to the subject—i.e., what this subject "means" to them—and who further take this design from geometry. By using an edge in place of a curve a unique tactual value is obtained.

Futurism is a glorification of personality. Every socalled "Futurist" has his own hobby; and there are almost as many kinds of painting as artists. For instance, one painter takes as his subject sounds, another, colours. A third goes back to old techniques; a fourth sees life through a magnifying glass; a fifth imposes an environment upon his subject proper, obtaining very startling effects; a sixth concerns himself purely with motion—in connection with which it is interesting to note the Japanese painters' wholly unrealistic rendering of the force of a river.

The painter Matisse has been called the greatest exponent of Cubist sculpture. At the 1913 exhibition the puzzled crowd in front of Brancusi's "Mlle. Pogany" was only rivalled by that which swarmed about the painting called "Nude Descending a Staircase." "Mlle. Pogany" consists of a more or less egg-shaped head with an unmistakable nose, and a sinuous suggestion of arms curving upward to the face. There is no differentiation in modelling affording even a hint of hands; in other words, the flow of line and volume is continuous. But what strikes the spectator at first glance, and focuses the attention throughout, is the enormous inscribed ovals, which everyone recognizes as the artist's conception of the subject's eyes. In this triumph of line for line's sake over realism we note the development of the basic principles of impressionism.

II.

Just as in the case of painting, it is a French school which brought new life to music; but at the same time, Germany has the honour of producing one of the greatest originators and masters of realism, Richard Strauss.

The modern French school of music finds its inspiration in the personal influence of César Franck. Debussy, Ravel and Satie all owe much to this great Belgian, who (like Maeterlinck and Verhaeren), was essentially a man of their own artistic nationality.

It is safe to say that there will always be somebody who still refuses to accept modernism in music; quoting in his defense the sovereign innovator, Beethoven! On a par with the sensation produced by the painting and sculpture of the Futurist variety was the excitement which the music of Strauss and Debussy first produced upon audiences. At present, Debussy threatens to become at any moment vulgarly common; while Strauss is fatuous in his clarity beside Schönberg; who, with Stravinsky, is the only god left by the public for the worship of the aesthetes.

Erik Satie is, in many respects, the most interesting of all modern composers. Nearly a quarter of a century ago he was writing what is now considered modern music. The most striking aspect of Satie's art is the truly extraordinary sense of humour which prompts one of his subjects, the "sea cucumber," to console himself philosophically for his lack of tobacco.

The "Five Orchestral Pieces" of Arnold Schonberg continue to be the leading sensation of the present-day musical world. Their composer occupies a position in many respects similar to that of the author of the "Nude Descending a Staircase." I do not in the least mean to ridicule Schönberg—no lawlessness could ever have produced such compositions as his, which resemble bristling forests contorted by irresistible winds. His work is always the expression of something mysteriously terrible—which is probably why Boston laughed.

I have purposely left until the last the greatest theorist of modern music—Scriabin. Logically, he belongs beside Stravinsky, as leader of the Russian school. But it is by means of Scriabin that we may most readily pass from music to literature, through the medium of what has been called "sense-transference," as exemplified by the colour music of the "Prometheus."

This "Poem of Fire" is the consummation of Scriabin's genius. To quote the *Transcript:* "At the first performance, by the Russian Symphony Society, on March 20, for the first time in history a composer used a chromatic color score in combination with orchestration. . . . At the beginning of the orchestration, a gauze rectangle in about the position of a picture suspended on the back wall became animated by flowing and blending colours. These colours were played by a 'colour-organ' or 'chromola,' having a keyboard with fifteen keys, and following a written score."

III.

The suggestion of an analogy between colour and music leads us naturally to the last branch of the New Art—to wit, literature. Only the most extreme cases will be discussed, such as have important bearing upon the very latest conceptions of artistic expression.

I will quote three contemporary authors to illustrate different phases and different degrees of the literary parallel to sound painting—in a rather faint hope that the first two may prepare the way for an appreciation of the third. First Amy Lowell's "Grotesque" affords a clear illustration of development from the ordinary to the abnormal.

Why do the lilies goggle their tongues at me
When I pluck them;
And writhe and twist,
And strangle themselves against my fingers,
So that I can hardly weave the garland
For your hair?
Why do they shriek your name
And spit at me
When I would cluster them?
Must I kill them
To make them lie still,
And send you a wreathe of lolling corpses
To turn putrid and soft
On your forehead
While you dance?

In this interesting poem we seem to discern something beyond the conventional. The lilies are made to express hatred by the employment of grotesque images. But there is nothing original in the pathetic fallacy. No one quarrels with Tennyson's lines.

There has fallen a splendid tear
From the passion-flower at the gate—

Let us proceed further—only noting in the last three lines that brutality which is typical of the New Art—and consider the following poem by the same author:

THE LETTER

Little cramped words scrawling all over the paper
Like draggled fly's legs,
What can you tell of the flaring moon
Through the oak leaves?
Or of an uncurtained window, and the bare floor
Spattered with moonlight?
Your silly quirks and twists have nothing in them
Of blossoming hawthorns.
And this paper is chill, crisp, smooth, virgin of loveliness
Beneath my hand.
I am tired, Beloved, of chafing my heart against
The want of you;

248

Of squeezing it into little ink drops,
And posting it.
And I scald alone, here under the fire
Of the great moon.

This poem is superb of its kind. I know of no image in all realistic writing which can approach the absolute vividness of the first two lines. The metaphor of the chafed heart is worthy of any poet; but its fanciful development would have been impossible in any literature except this ultramodern.

I shall now quote from a sonnet by my second author, Donald Evans:

Her voice was fleet-limbed and immaculate,
And like peach blossoms blown across the wind

Her white words made the hour seem cool and kind,
Hung with soft dawns that danced a shadow fête.
A silken silence crept up from the South.
The flutes were hushed that mimed the orange moon,
And down the willow stream my sighs were strewn,
While I knelt to the corners of her mouth.

In the figure "Her voice was fleet-limbed," and the phrase "white words," we have a sought-for literary parallel to the work of the "sound painters." It is interesting to compare Dante's expressions of a precisely similar nature, occurring in the first and fifth cantos, respectively, of the Inferno—"dove il Sol tace," and "in loco d'ogni luce muto."

From Donald Evans to Gertrude Stein is a natural step—up or down, and one which I had hoped the first two might enable us to take in security. Gertrude Stein subordinates the meaning of words to the beauty of the words themselves. Her art is the logic of literary sound painting carried to its extreme. While we must admit that it is logic, must we admit that it is art?

Having prepared the way, so far as it is possible, for a just appreciation, I now do my best to quote from the book "Tender Buttons," as follows:

(1)   A sound
    Elephants beaten with candy and little pops and

chews all bolts and reckless reckless rats, this
is this.

(2)   Salad Dressing and an Artichoke
Please pale hot, please cover rose, please acre in the
red stranger, please butter all the beef-steak
with regular feel faces.

(3)   Suppose an Eyes

• • •

Go red go red, laugh white.
Suppose a collapse is rubbed purr, is rubbed purr get.
Little sales ladies little sales ladies little saddles of
mutton.
Little sales of leather and such beautiful, beautiful,
beautiful beautiful.

The book from which these selections are drawn is unques-
tionably a proof of great imagination on the part of the author-
ess, as anyone who tries to imitate her work will discover for
himself. Here we see traces of realism, similar to those which
made the "Nude Descending a Staircase" so baffling. As far as
these "Tender Buttons" are concerned, the sum and substance
of criticism is impossible. The unparalleled familiarity of the
medium precludes its use for the purpose of aesthetic effect.
And here, in their logical conclusion, impressionistic tendencies
are reduced to absurdity.

The question now arises, how much of all this is really Art?

The answer is: we do not know. The great men of the future
will most certainly profit by the experimentation of the present
period. An insight into the unbroken chain of artistic develop-
ment during the last half century disproves the theory that
modernism is without foundation; rather we are concerned with
a natural unfolding of sound tendencies. That the conclusion
is, in a particular case, absurdity, does not in any way impair
the value of the experiment, so long as we are dealing with
sincere effort. The New Art, maligned though it may be by
fakirs and fanatics, will appear in its essential spirit to the
unprejudiced critic as a courageous and genuine exploration of
untrodden ways.

Harvard Advocate, June 1915.

To John Dos Passos

[4 Patchin Place
April 12, 1930]

pleasant weather,Columbus!

'twas even more than a pleasure to read The NR#p
239 sixth 1 from top quotes THE MECHANISM OF
THE THEATER ... THE MECHANISM OF THE
CIRCUS IS MASKED close quotes   welwellwelll
perhaps Not lasciate ogni speranza Afterallll!

Ye Wear-ne'er hath paxvobiscumbed elsewherishly*viz parry
an burlin en root to the amen soviet yeastcake;he wanted i to go
but $,if not sens forebad.   Am almost thru eheuing & reddy to
sing "Whan that Ap Reely"
we hope to see yousesboths verysoon,Mudumunmushoo!
                                        lay khyeu mangz
        nbps) Q;Whence the phrase "virgin forest"? A;Only G-d
        can make a tree
                        Anon.(20thC American)
        #issue graphically recommended by Sir Silbert Geldes
        this day of grace 4/12/30
                        *loaning us a Lachaise
                        HugeHead and Drawing plus
                        several Kuhns(and a Cummings

(From   HATS OFF to thea orthodox flea,
the   who attempted to bugger a bee
Sanscrit)   But eamerged from thea fray
               in a familea way . . .
               which is why wea do things so fee-blea

The Adult, the Artist
and the Circus

When something joyous, which made our childhood particularly worth while, fails to delight us as adults, we go through the apparently serene process of assuming a lofty attitude toward the "outgrown" pleasure. Upon close inspection, however, this process proves to be far from serene. Take our grown-up disdain of the circus, for instance. What actually happens, from the moment when the circus first occurs to us until the moment when we dismiss it as "childish," is nothing less than a BATTLE.

For, at the very thought of "circus," a swarm of long-imprisoned desires breaks jail. Armed with beauty and demanding justice and everywhere threatening us with curiosity and Spring and childhood, this mob of forgotten wishes begins to storm the supposedly impregnable fortifications of our Present. We are caught off our guard—we must defend ourselves somehow: any weapon will do. We seize the idea that a circus is nothing but a big and colourful toy especially invented for the amusement of undeveloped or naif minds. With this idea and the idea that the theatre is an enlightened form of entertainment worthy of our mature intelligences, we lay about us wildly; until—after a brave struggle—the motley horde retreats, abandoning its dead and wounded. But we ourselves are not unscathed: our wounds give us no peace; we must somehow forget them. Accordingly we betake ourselves to a theatre or to the movies. There, under the influence of a powerful anaesthetic known as Pretend, we forget not only the circus but all our other sorrows, including the immortal dictum of that inexorable philosopher Krazy Kat: *It's what's behind me that I am.*

But suppose, now, that an exciting experiment is attempted. Why not try to consider the circus directly, or as a self-sufficient phenomenon independent of the theater, movies, radio and similar lofty amusements? I have in mind neither a detailed analysis of the American circus of today, nor yet a pompous monologue on the circus throughout the ages, but merely a few personal remarks anent the menagerie, the freaks, and the "big show" of the Ringling Brothers and Barnum & Bailey circus.

And speaking of the menagerie, nothing can shake my conviction that a periodic and highly concentrated dose of wild animals—elephants, tigers, lions, leopards, jaguars, bears, wolves, giraffes, kangaroo, zebras, horned horses, camels, hyenas, rhinoceri and at least one hippopotamus—is indispensable to the happiness of all mature civilized human beings. Were Congress to pass a bill compelling every adult inhabitant of the United States of America to visit the circus at least twice a year, with the stipulation that each visitor must spend (willy-nilly) not less than half an hour in the menagerie, I believe that, throughout the entire country, four out of five hospitals, jails and insane-asylums would close down. It is my hunch that, as an immediate result of this simple legislation, hundreds of cripples—lame, halt and blind—would toss their infirmities to the winds, thousands of ill-starred homes would break into paeans of rejoicing—and millions of psychoanalysts would be thrown out of employment.

For the benefit of any disciple of Freud who may chance to peruse the above statement, I hereby whisper that my own totem is the elephant. And what, gentle subscriber to *Vanity Fair*, may your totem be? In case you aren't sure, or think you haven't any, I counsel you to take the very next train for whatever city the circus may happen to occupy (unless you are so fortunate as to have it with you at the moment). Above all, don't be satisfied with a trip to some mere zoo; for zoos—poor, placid, colourless things that they are—completely lack that outrageous intensity which makes the circus menagerie unique as a curative institution and endows the denizens of that institution with a fourth- or fifth-dimensional significance for the neuroses.

By this time, surely, my worthy readers have doubtless decided that I myself am a salaried member of that branch of the circus which comprises "the strange people." Although this is an error—although I am neither a Missing Link nor a Fat Lady nor yet an Ambassador from Mars—I may mention that

253

I feel highly complimented at being mistaken for one or all of these prodigies. For (in my opinion) happy is that writer, who, in the course of his lifetime, succeeds in making a dozen persons react to his personality as genuinely or vividly as millions react, each and every year, to the magnetic personality of Zip, the What-Is-It! Nor can I refrain, at this point, saluting also the Giant, the Pygmy, the Pin-Head, the unutterably refined Human Skeleton and the other distinguished members of Zip's very select society. Having done this, I shall spare my readers further rhapsody. In return for the favor, I ask that all who are interested in a sensitive interpretation of certain world-famous oddities, as well as in the origin of what we now call the American circus, will hasten to consult (if by mischance they have not already done so) M. R. Werner's excellent and extremely entertaining biography: *Barnum.*

Having cast rapid glances at the menagerie and the freaks, we enter "the big top"—where dwells the really-truly circus-show. This may be described as a gigantic spectacle; *which is surrounded by an audience*—in contrast to our modern theatres, where an audience and a spectacle merely confront each other. The show itself, we immediately notice, has a definite kind of bigness. By "definite kind," I mean that the bigness of the circus-show is intrinsic—like the bigness of an elephant or of a skyscraper—not superficial, as in the case of an enlarged snapshot. The nature of this bigness becomes apparent when we perceive that it is never, for so much as the fraction of an instant, motionless. Anyone who has stood just across the street from the Woolworth Building and has watched it wriggle upward like a skyrocket, or who has observed the irrevocably, gradually moving structure of an elephant which is "standing still"—anyone who has beheld these miracles, will understand me when I say the bigness of the circus-show is *a kind of mobility.* Movement is the very stuff out of which this dream is made. Or we may say that movement is the content, the subject matter, of the circus-show, while bigness is its form; provided we realize that here (as in all true "works of art") content and form are aspects of a homogeneous whole.

At this great spectacle, as nowhere else, the adult onlooker knows that unbelievably skilful and inexorably beautiful and unimaginably dangerous things are continually happening. But this is not all: he feels that there is a little too much going on at any given moment. Here and now, I desire to point out that *this is as it should be.* To the objection that the three-ring circus "creates such a confused impression," I beg to reply: "Speaking of confused impressions—how about the downrush of a first-rate roller coaster or the incomparable yearning of the Parisian *balançoirs à vapeur,* not to mention the solemn visit of a seventy-five centimetre projectile and the frivolous propinquity of Shrapnel?" For it is with thrilling experiences of a life-or-death order (including certain authentic "works of art"—and most emphatically *not* with going to the movies or putting out the cat) that the circus-show entirely belongs.

Within "the big top," as nowhere else on earth, is to be found Actuality. Living players play with living. There are no tears produced by onion-oil and Mr. Nevin's Rosary, no pasteboard hovels and *papier-mâché* palaces, no "cuts," "retakes," or "N.G.'s"—and no curtain calls after suicide. At positively every performance Death Himself lurks, glides, struts, breathes, is. Lest any agony be missing, a mob of clowns tumbles loudly in and out of that inconceivably sheer fabric of doom, whose beauty seems endangered by the spectator's least heartbeat or whisper. As for the incredible and living designs, woven in this fabric by animal trainers, equestrians, acrobats— they are immune to forgetfulness in the same way that certain paintings, poems and musical compositions are immune. Although it was only once, and twenty-odd years ago, that my eyes had the extraordinary honour to behold a slight young man whose first name was DANGER DERIDING DEATH DEFYING DESPERATE DAREDEVIL DIAVOLO LOOPS THE LOOP ON A BICYCLE (his last name being, if I am not mistaken, PORTHOS: LEAPS THE GAP OVER FIVE ELEPHANTS), I have not forgotten this person and shall never forget him, simply because he was a great artist—who, like Paul Cézanne, died the most fortunate and illustrious of deaths: died at the *motif,* and in the execution of his art.

So, *un*gentle reader, (as you and I value what we should be ashamed—after witnessing a few minor circus-marvels—to call our "lives,") let us never be fooled into taking seriously that perfectly superficial distinction which is vulgarly drawn between the circus-show and "art" or "the arts." Let us not forget that every authentic "work of art" is in and of itself alive and that, however "the arts" may differ among themselves, their common function is the expression of that supreme aliveness which is known as "beauty." This being so, our three-ring circus is art—for to contend that the spectacle in question is not an authentic manifestation of "beauty" is as childish, as to dismiss the circus on the ground that it is "childish," is idiotic.

In closing, the present writer wishes to state (1) that an extremely intimate connection exists between Con Colleanos' forward somersault (from and to a wire in mid-air) and Homer's Odyssey (2) that a sure method of understanding Igor Stravinsky's *Le Sacre du Printemps*, is to study the voluminous precision and fugual delicacy of Mr. Ringling's "Ponderous Pachyderms under the direction of the greatest of all animal trainers" (3) that El Greco, in painting, and "Ernest Clark, in his triple somersaulting double-twisting and reverse flights through space" give strikingly similar performances, and (4) that the fluent technique of seals and of sea lions comprises certain untranslatable idioms, certain innate flexions, which astonishingly resemble the spiritual essence of poetry.

Vanity Fair, October 1925.

CONEY ISLAND

Although it is true that the inhabitants of the U.S.A. have ample cause for pessimism, thanks to Bad Art, Bootleggery and 26,000 lesser degrees of Bunk, it is also true that said inhabitants are the fortunate possessors of a perfectly genuine panacea. Were not this so, throughout the breadth and length of our fair land mayhem would magnify itself to prodigious proportions, burglary would bulge to deadly dimensions, policemen would populate our most secret sanctuaries and such notable nodes of *Kultur* as New York City would leap *en masse* to the celestial regions. Unbelievable as it may appear, there might even come a day when not a single campanulate congressman went to sleep on duty and not a single authentic artist starved at his Corona. In short (and to put it very mildly) anything might happen.

But the panacea is genuine. Crime, accordingly, is kept within quite convenient bounds, murder is monotonously punished, unart and nonliquor exchange visiting cards and the dollar bill waves triumphant o'er the land of the free and the home of the slave—all of which is due to the existence of an otherwise not important island, whose modest name would seem to suggest nothing more obstreperous than the presence of rabbits. No wonder learned people state that we occupy an epoch of miracles!

At the outset, one thing should be understood: it is not owing to sociological, political, or even psychological predilections that the present and unlearned writer partakes of the cure in question. Quite the contrary. Like those millions of other so-called human beings who find relief for their woes, each and every year, at Coney Island, he occupies these miraculous premises with purely personal intentions—or, more explicitly, in order to have a good time. And a good time he has. Only when his last spendable dime has irretrievably disappeared and his face sadly is turned toward his dilatory domicile, does it so much as occur to your humble servant to plumb the significance of his recent experiences. Such being the case, there can be no reasonable doubt as to his intellectual honesty *re* the isle and its amusements, concerning which (for the benefit of all thoroughly unbenighted persons and an unhappy few who are not accustomed to lose their complexes on The Thunderbolt) he hereby begs to discourse.

The incredible temple of pity and terror, mirth and amazement, which is popularly known as Coney Island, really constitutes a perfectly unprecedented fusion of the circus and the theatre. It resembles the theatre, in that it fosters every known species of illusion. It suggests the circus, in that it puts us in touch with whatever is hair-raising, breath-taking and pore-opening. But Coney has a distinct drop on both theatre and circus. Whereas at the theatre we merely are deceived, at Coney we deceive ourselves. Whereas at the circus we are merely spectators of the impossible, at Coney we ourselves perform impossible feats—we turn all the heavenly somersaults imaginable and dare all the delirious dangers conceivable; and when, rushing at horrid velocity over irrevocable precipices, we beard the force of gravity in his lair, no acrobat, no lion tamer, can compete with us.

Be it further stated that humanity (and, by the way, there is such a thing) is most emphatically itself at Coney. Whoever, on a really hot day, has attempted to swim three strokes in Coney Island waters will be strongly inclined to believe that nowhere else in all of the round world is humanity quite so much itself. (We have reference to the noteworthy phenomenon that every Coney Island swimmer swims, not in the water, but in the populace.) Nor is this spontaneous itselfness, on the part of Coney Island humanity, merely aquatic. It is just as much terrestrial and just as much aerial. Anybody who, of a truly scorching Saturday afternoon, has been caught in a Coney Island jam will understand the terrestrial aspect, and anybody who has watched (let alone participated in) a Coney Island roller coaster will comprehend the aerial aspect, of humanity's irreparable itselfness. But this means that the *audience* of Coney Island—as well as the *performance* given by that unmitigated circus-theatre—is unique. . . .

Ask Freud, he knows.

Now to seek a formula for such a fundamental and glorious institution may appear, at first blush, presumptuous. Indeed, those of our readers who are dyed-in-the-wool Coney Island fans have doubtless resented our using the words "circus-theatre" to describe an (after all) indescribable phenomenon. We hasten to reassure them: Coney for us, as for themselves, is Coney and nothing else. But certain aspects of this miracle mesh, so to speak, with the theatre and with the circus; a fact which we consider strictly significant—not for Coney, but for art. We repeat: the essence of Coney Island's "circus-theatre" consists in *homogeneity*. THE AUDIENCE IS THE PERFOR-MANCE, and vice versa. If this be formula, let us make the most of it.

Those readers who have inspected the International Theatre Exposition will realize that the worldwide "new movement" in the theatre is toward a similar goal. Two facts are gradually being recognized: first, that the circus is an authentic "theatric" phenomenon, and second, that the conventional "theatre" is a box of negligible tricks. The existing relationships between actor and audience and theatre have been discovered to be rotten at their very cores. All sorts of new "theatres" having been suggested, to remedy this thoroughly disgraceful state of affairs—disgraceful because, in the present writer's own lingo, *all genuine theatre is a verb and not a noun*—we ourselves have the extraordinary honour to suggest: Coney Island. And lest anybody consider this suggestion futuristic, we will quote from *The Little Review* the suggestion of Enrico Prampolini, entitled (among other things):

THE ELECTRO-DYNAMIC POLY-
DIMENSIONAL ARCHITECTURE
OF LUMINOUS PLASTIC
ELEMENTS MOVING IN
THE CENTRE OF THE
THEATRICAL HOLLOW

This novel *theatrical construction*, owing to its position, allows the enlargement of the *visual angle* of perspective beyond the horizon, displacing it on top and vice versa in a simultaneous interpenetration, towards a centrifugal irradiation of infinite visual and emotional angles of scenic action.

THE POLYDIMENSIONAL SCENIC SPACE, THE NEW FUTURISTIC CREATION for the theatre to come, opens new worlds for the magic and technique of the theatre.

Amen. . . .

Vanity Fair, June 1926.

Seven Samples of
Dramatic Criticism

I. Boom Boomed

How Much Assassination is a play which is surely worth going to see. My throat specialist was particularly moved, and spent half the last appointment describing to me exactly why the production is a human document. As nearly as I can make out, I agree with him; although it seems he was in the air forces. No one who ever went over the top, which neither of us did, can fail to be amused by the dialogue between Rinehart and Belasco, or is it between Buffalo Bill and General Pershing? We forget which, unfortunately. Anyhow, the idea is there; and that man who did the ape in *All God's Chillun Got Wings* is a remarkable actor in every way, and some of the slang just makes you want to stand up and say, "Let there be no more war!"

II. Claptrap Bearnaise

Pink Thunder from start to finish is a gripping melodrama in which frankly tropical lust is forcefully contrasted with intrinsic spiritual affection. The action—which reaches a heart-rending climax on the summit of Popocatepetl—is essentially a struggle between two women, one of whom is certainly no worse than she should be, for the possession of Peter Thomson, a missionary who is torn by conflicting emotions. Thrill-ridden scenes succeed each other with an agonizing rapidity, until Lucille Stingray (played to almost unendurable perfection by Mischa Elman) bribes a bloodthirsty tribe of Peruvian headhunters to abduct the sleeping heroine, for whom, until this dreadful moment, Peter—absorbed in the excruciating convolutions of his own ubiquitous conscience—had cherished merely a vague, unrecognizable emotion. The crisis, however, precipitates love; and the apostle is supplanted by the man. In a delirium of perspicuity, scarce knowing what he does, Michael Arlen as Peter rescues Isabel who faints with pleasure in his arms: whereupon, overcome—in what would appear to be the supreme moment of his life—by mingled inhibitions, the young man turns his back on temptation, gives himself (in an agony of remorse) to Lucille, and promptly jumps into the infernal fires of the volcano, which go out, causing the superstitious aborigines to hail him as a god. This sacrilege brings the devotee to his true senses—a fascinating psychological twist, for which the author (Miss Marianne Moore) is to be unstintingly congratulated—and he immediately, to everyone's relief, inherits sixteen million dollars, kisses June Walker, embraces the American flag, and lives happily ever after as innumerable spectators swarmingly exeunt from New York's best ventilated theatre.

III. Strut Your Stuff

Strut Your Stuff is a typical revue with Ethel Barrymore and the costumes—consisting of paper napkins, accurately and painstakingly designed by Claude Bragdon, beautifully photographed by Alfred Stieglitz, and capably produced by Edward Royce.

IV. Love's Coming of Age

Hairy Jones' *Desire under the Elms* is a play in the manner of Greek tragedy about a monkey who is also a Negro in which little is left to the imagination. Hairy Jones (not to be confused with Robert Edmond Jones who did his level best with the somewhat slanting elms) after being born (in New England) becomes "dif'rent." During all the rather long next, or third, act, the heroine alternately dabbles in incest and hides peanuts under a rug to amuse her doting grandfather who, we are given to understand, hangs himself in a shop window on the corner of Fifth Avenue and 42nd Street to the dulcet thuddings of a tom-tom, as the curtain falls and subscribers exchange looks all over the Provincetown Theatre. But this is not the point of the production by any means, for the author is far from being one whom mere mute inglorious melodrama satisfies. Rather are we presented with a continuous cross section of the Oedipus complex as it occurs in a mixture of the African galley slave with the gorilla who has become a typical citizen of New Bedford, Massachusetts, during those old whaling days when might made wrong. The cast is excellent, Mary Garden excelling in the difficult part of Liz, while Sir Al Forbes-Robertson Jolson's portrayal of the ambigeneric hero is a triumph of tact, vigour, and nuance; and profusely illustrated brochures, entitled "Anthony Comstock's Reminiscences, or Tramping on Life" are distributed (gratis) to members of the audience, at each and every performance which I myself enjoyed very much.

V. The Great American Drama at Last

Mickey's Yiddisher Tulip: Several million dollars have already flowed into the ermine-lined pocketbook of her who is, to put it mildly, the authoress of *Mickey's Yiddisher Tulip,* and small wonder! For sheer blitheness of sentiment, gaiety of situation, sublimity of pathos, and general inventiveness, no story, since *Uncle Tom's Cabin* thrilled our immediate ancestors, has enshrined so many genuinely laughable and authentically weepable moments, making of the human heart a sensitive and responsive instrument at the beck and call of alternate terror and joy. It were indeed difficult to imagine what could be more wholly touching, and at the same time funnier, than a juxtaposition of the Icelandic and Assyrian temperaments; yet precisely this feat has won for the inspired progenitor of *Mickey's Yiddisher Tulip* an everlasting seat among the geniuses of all time. (Standing room only.)

VI. Corn Beef and Caviar

Once again, after its triumphant tour of Athens, Constantinople, and Pekin, *The Bohemian Ballet* is with us. The only fault which your reviewer can find with this invariably extraordinary ballet organization, whose ranks are this year enriched by two dancers of international renown—Gretchen Fahrenheit and Mike Frost—is that it somehow just misses being neither the Swedish nor yet the Russian Ballet. Nevertheless, there are some far from wholly unpleasant moments; as when, for example, the superb curtain by Wable Wicasse falls (after the third scene of *La Princesse Enceinte* is somewhat less than half over) on the by no means negligible occiput of Igor Ivanovich Vladimir Skipski; or when Lucy Goeblum (that most astute of Lithu-anian *terpsichoristes*) executes the banana dance of the Fiji Islands to a witty, if slightly posthumous, nocturne by Chopin—or during those few utterly inspired, absolutely unforgettable instants, when, against the molecular meander-ings of Strapfka Fooking, are agreeably silhouetted the cerebral somersaults of Serge Kapoot.

VII. Pollyanna Aesthetics

The Black Suspenders is, as its name frankly implies, an evanes-cent folk tale of corrupt peasant life done into verse by Edna St. Vincent Millay and translated from the Algerian by Mrs. John F. Hylan. George Smith, the hero, ably interpreted by Mr. John Howard Lawson, is put to sleep by a fairy named Sylvio, and remains in a state of coma during the entire perfor-mance, parts of which (especially the twelfth and twenty-sixth tableaux) might be omitted to advantage without violating the delicate spirit of Arthur Hopkins' conception. Aside from this minor error, the plot deals with Smith's subconscious reaction to three characters—Geraldine Glumb, a future mother; Doro-thy Dumb, a telephone girl, and Creichton Crumb, a painter of marine animals—all of whom are obviously in search of the author, Yudenich Pilsudski Numb, who remains off-stage, however, occasionally singing *Nearer My God To Thee* to the accompaniment of an ancient African instrument shaped some-what like a cross between a beggar on horseback and the mando-lute. An audience (composed, last Saturday night, of a sprinkling of Danish plumbers and a scattering of Norwegian bank messengers) loudly booed the far from discreditable work of Philip Widget Moeller in the role of Philip Moeller Widget, and expressed almost unjustified approval whenever—as not infrequently happens—Geraldine hits Creichton with a stuffed cat in the middle of Dorothy's wedding. On the whole, we are reluctantly forced to admit, we can congratulate Miss Millay, Mr. Pilsudski Numb and Mayoress Hylan.

Vanity Fair, May 1925.

SELF=PREFACES

Stein who had been much impressed by The Enor-
mous Room *said that Cummings did not copy, he was
the natural heir of the New England tradition with its
aridity and its sterility, but also with its individuality.*
　　　　—*Gertrude Stein,* The Autobiography of Alice B.
　　　　　　　　　　　　　　　　　　　Toklas *(1933)*

Few poets have introduced their own work and purposes, not
only in language but in art, as stylishly and concisely as Cum-
mings. He worked excerpts from several prefaces into the fourth
of his Charles Eliot Norton lectures at Harvard in 1952 (collected
as *i: Six Nonlectures* [1953]). Wittily entitled "i & you & is," this
is his fullest esthetic self-presentation. His preface to the 1958
edition of *Eimi* (1933), really among the most extraordinary sin-
gle prefaces in American literature, demonstrates that even in his
final years Cummings had experimental designs, which is to say
that he never doubled back on his more radical self. (Were this a
bigger book, it too would be here.) He additionally wrote intro-
ductions to his visual art. The last preface reprinted here accounts
for the title of his collection, *No Thanks* (1935), acknowledging
as it does all the publishers previously rejecting the manuscript,
Cummings typically revealing that professional guts necessarily
complements esthetic courage.

To Ezra Pound

6 Wyman Road
Cambridge, Mass.
October 24 1952

& right ye were,Ezree meee by,to communicate the Wil-liamsiana which arrived this day,forwarded from nh:& glad-dened my spouse&self

now this dame "Cummins" has(as you doubtless know) been after eec for yarz;so am selfishly-delighted she's attacking someone else(poor shawn shay)

but regret to learn our laymyspiritatherfeetfull acquaintance has injured his Amongmanyothers,undistinguished cote(w-ith a circumflex). What was he up or down or sideways or neither to,pray?

am in good hands here,belonging to 1 "John Finley";profess-ing Greek,extolling Humanities,&(tactfully not when I'm around;however)praising O'Possumtotheskies. A nice—the JF—fellow. Has already preserved me from well nigh not numerable "social" phenómena:&(this in thine oreille)will, j'espere,make possible a big escape to ny circa Xmas!

we live in a little house,far from seive lies ation;& a big BLUEJAY seems to be our chief mascot—a stalwart rascal, whose Hue give me Joy unmitigated;& who fears no crow or gull extant. I've already remembered him to you

Marion sends love to yourself & Dorothy! Please keep many fingers crossed(on my nonworthy bewhole)from 8 to 9 PM this coming Tuesday,28th October;my 1st "Norton lecture"
—oop thih rubbles

l'enfant prodigue

WILLIAMSIANA. A woman named Virginia Kent Cummins had attacked the Library of Congress for appointing William Carlos Williams consultant in poetry. Williams' verse, said Mrs. Cummins, was "the very voice of Communism." Pound sent Cummings an account of the incident that he had clipped from the *Washington Times Herald*.

JOHN FINLEY. Professor of Classics at Harvard, where Cummings lectured in 1952–53.

Nonlecture Four: i & you & is

Now comes, from my point of view, the excitement; and from yours, in all likelihood, the boredom—egocentrically supposing the boredom didn't come long ago. For I herewith assume (if possible even more egocentrically) that when we last met, or didn't meet, a certain longlost personage became EECummings: thereby reducing the aesthetic selfportrait of one whole half of this not divisible ignoramus to an exploration of his stance as a writer.

Writing, I feel, is an art; and artists, I feel, are human beings. As a human being stands, so a human being is: not that some human beings aren't acrobats, while others—but why anticipate Him and Santa Claus? Suffice it to say that the present non-poetical period will consist of nothing but sentences, essays, and parts of essays, all of which express a standing human being. I shall take these expressions chronologically; stating when they were published and how, but letting you draw your own (if any) conclusions. Over- and under-standing will make their appearance later: during the next thirty minutes, a particular human being will merely stand for thirty years.

1922—from my first published book, The Enormous Room

> There are certain things in which one is unable to believe for the simple reason that he never ceases to feel them. Things of this sort—things which are always inside of us and in fact are us and which consequently will not be pushed off or away where we can begin thinking about them—are no longer things;they,and the us which they are,equals A Verb;an IS.

1926—from the foreword to a book of poems called Is 5

> On the assumption that my technique is either complicated or original or both,the publishers have politely requested me to write an introduction to this book.

At least my theory of technique,if I have one,is very far from original;nor is it complicated. I can express it in fifteen words,by quoting The Eternal Question And Immortal Answer of burlesk,viz. "Would you hit a woman with a child?—No,I'd hit her with a brick." Like the burlesk comedian,I am abnormally fond of that precision which creates movement.

If a poet is anybody,he is somebody to whom things made matter very little—somebody who is obsessed by Making . . .

Ineluctable preoccupation with The Verb gives a poet one priceless advantage:whereas nonmakers must content themselves with the merely undeniable fact that two times two is four,he rejoices in an irresistible truth(to be found,in abbreviated costume, upon the title page of the prevent volume)

1927—An Imaginary Dialogue Between An Author And A Public, printed on the book-jacket of my first play

Author: Well?
Public: What is Him about?
Author: Why ask me? Did I or didn't I make the play?
Public: But surely you know what you're making—
Author: Beg pardon,Mr. Public;I surely make what I'm knowing.
Public: So far as I'm concerned,my very dear sir,nonsense isn't everything in life.
Author: And so far as you're concerned "life" is a verb of two voices—active,to do,and passive,to dream. Others believe doing to be only a kind of dreaming. Still others have discovered (in a mirror surrounded with mirrors),something harder than silence but softer than falling;the third voice of "life",which believes itself and which cannot mean because it is.
Public: Bravo,but are such persons good for anything in particular?
Author: They are good for nothing but walking upright in the cordial revelation of the fatal reflexive.

Public: And your play is all about one of these persons,Mr. Author?

Author: Perhaps. But(let me tell you a secret)I rather hope my play is one of these persons.

1933—from my Soviet Russian diary, EIMI

Not to completely feel is thinking . . .

to grow is a fate.

People may dare to live,people may be taught or may teach themselves death;noone can learn growing. Noone can dare to grow. Growing equals that any reason or motive or unreason becomes every other unreason or reason or motive. Here exists no sign,no path,no distance,and no time . . . Drunk and becauseless(talking about a cyclone,telling how at last with the disappearance even of impossibility himself found actually himself and suddenly becoming the cyclone;not perishing and not surviving;Being) the poet Hart Crane was able to invent growth's likeness.

1934—from an introduction written for the Modern Library edition of The Enormous Room

When this book wrote itself,I was observing a negligible portion of something incredibly more distant than any sun;something more unimaginably huge than the most prodigious of all universes—
Namely?
The Individual.

Russia,I felt,was more deadly than war:when nationalists hate,they hate by merely killing and maiming human beings;when internationalists hate,they hate by categorying and pigeonholing human beings.

Eimi is the individual again;a more complex individual,a more enormous room.

1938—from an introduction written for my miscalled Collected Poems; thrice miscalled, since three books of poems (entitled 50 Poems, One Times One, and XAIPE) have already followed it

Take the matter of being born. What does being born mean to mostpeople? Catastrophe unmitigated. Social revolution . . . Mostpeople fancy a guaranteed birthproof safetysuit of nondestructible selflessness. If mostpeople were to be born twice they'd improbably call it dying—

you and I are not snobs. We can never be born enough. We are human beings;for whom birth is a supremely welcome mystery,the mystery of growing:the mystery which happens only and whenever we are faithful to ourselves . . . Life,for eternal us,is now . . .

What their most synthetic not to mention transparent majesty,mrsandmr collective foetus,would improbably call a ghost is walking . . . He is a healthily complex,a naturally homogeneous, citizen of immortality . . . He is a little more than everything,he is democracy;he is alive: he is ourselves.

. . . Nothing believed or doubted . . .

Always the beautiful answer who asks a more beautiful question

Here let me, momentarily interrupting my egocentric self, read you a pitying and terrible passage from the New Testament; on which our next selection (one of a pair of essays concerning Ezra Pound) is based. Most of you are no doubt acquainted with this more than most famous manifestation of whatever I can only call feeling—as against unfeeling: alias knowing and believing and thinking—this masterpoem of human perception, whose seventh verse alone exterminates all conventional morality

Jesus went unto the mount of Olives.

And early in the morning he came again into the temple, and all the people came until him; and he sat down, and taught them.

And the scribes and Pharisees brought unto him a woman taken in adultery; and when they had set her in the midst,

They say unto him, Master, this woman was taken in adultery, in the very act.

Now Moses in the law commanded us, that such should be stoned: but what sayest thou?

This they said, tempting him, that they might have to accuse him. But Jesus stooped down, and with his finger wrote on the ground, as though he heard them not.

So when they continued asking him, he lifted up himself, and said unto them, He that is without sin among you, let him first cast a stone at her.

And again he stooped down, and wrote on the ground.

And they which heard it, being convicted by their own conscience, went out one by one, beginning at the eldest, even unto the last: and Jesus was left alone, and the woman standing in the midst.

When Jesus had lifted up himself, and saw none but the woman, he said unto her, Woman, where are those thine accusers? hath no man condemned thee?

She saith, No man, Lord. And Jesus said unto her, Neither do I condemn thee: go, and sin no more.

Follows my essay—Anno Domini 1940—written at the request of Miss Frances Steloff, and published in her Gotham Book Mart catalogue entitled We Moderns

John,viii,7.

So now let us talk about something else. This is a free country because compulsory education. This is a free country because nobody has to eat. This is a free country because not any other country was is or ever will be free. So now you know and knowledge is power.

An interesting fact when you come right down to it is that simple people like complex things. But what amounts to an extraordinary coincidence is mediocre people liking firstrate things. The explanation can't be because complex things are simple. It must be because mediocre people are firstrate.

So now let us pull the wool over each other's toes and go to Hell. John,viii,7.

1944—an essay prefacing the catalogue of an exhibition of my paintings at the American British Art Center, New York City; but whose subject isn't the art of painting and is Art Herself. In this essay, four words—"good," "bad," "war," "peace"—are surrounded by quotationmarks whenever they occur.

Simple people,people who don't exist,prefer things which don't exist,simple things.

"Good" and "bad" are simple things. You bomb me = "bad." I bomb you = "good." Simple people(who,incidentally,run this socalled world)know this(they know everything)whereas complex people—people who feel something—are very,very ignorant and really don't know anything.

Nothing,for simple knowing people,is more dangerous than ignorance. Why?

Because to feel something is to be alive.

"War" and "peace" are not dangerous or alive:far from it. "Peace" is the inefficiency of science. "War" is the science of inefficiency. And science is knowing and knowing is measuring.

Ignorant people really must be educated;that is,they must be made to stop feeling something,and compelled to begin knowing or measuring everything. Then(then only)they won't threaten the very nonexistence of what all simple people call civilization.

Very luckily for you and me,the uncivilized sun mysteri-
ously shines on "good" and "bad" alike. He is an artist.

Art is a mystery.

A mystery is something immeasurable.

In so far as every child and woman and man may be
immeasurable,art is the mystery of every man and woman
and child. In so far as a human being is an artist,skies and
mountains and oceans and thunderbolts and butterflies are
immeasurable;and art is every mystery of nature. Nothing
measurable can be alive;nothing which is not alive can be
art;nothing which cannot be art is true:and everything untrue
doesn't matter a very good God damn . . .

item:it is my complex hope that the pictures here exhibited
are neither "good" nor "bad",neither peacelike nor warful—
that(on the contrary)they are living.

1945—a contribution to Charles Norman's "symposium"
(which sold out one issue of the shortlived newspaper PM) con-
cerning this selfstyled world's greatest and most generous liter-
ary figure: who had just arrived at our nation's capitol, attired
in half a GI uniform and ready to be hanged as a traitor by the
only country which ever made even a pretense of fighting for
freedom of speech

Re Ezra Pound—poetry happens to be an art;and artists
happen to be human beings.

An artist doesn't live in some geographical abstraction,su-
perimposed on a part of this beautiful earth by the nonimagi-
nation of unanimals and dedicated to the proposition that
massacre is a social virtue because murder is an individual
vice. Nor does an artist live in some soi-disant world,nor does
he live in some socalled universe,nor does he live in any num-
ber of "worlds" or in any number of "universes". As for a
few trifling delusions like the "past" and "present" and
"future" of quote mankind unquote,they may be big enough
for a couple of billion supermechanized submorons but
they're much too small for one human being.

274

Every artist's strictly illimitable country is himself.

An artist who plays that country false has committed suicide;and even a good lawyer cannot kill the dead. But a human being who's true to himself—whoever himself may be—is immortal;and all the atomic bombs of all the antiartists in spacetime will never civilize immortality.

Also 1945—from an essay contributed to Oscar Williams' anthology called The War Poets

when you confuse art with propaganda,you confuse an act of God with something which can be turned on and off like the hot water faucet. If "God" means nothing to you(or less than nothing)I'll cheerfully substitute one of your own favorite words,"freedom". You confuse freedom—the only freedom—with absolute tyranny . . .

all over this socalled world,hundreds of millions of servile and insolent inhuman unbeings are busily rolling and unrolling in the enlightenment of propaganda. So what? There are still a few erect human beings in the socalled world. Proudly and humbly,I say to these human beings:

"O my fellow citizens,many an honest man believes a lie. Though you are as honest as the day,fear and hate the liar. Fear and hate him when he should be feared and hated:now. Fear and hate him where he should be feared and hated:in yourselves.

"Do not hate and fear the artist in yourselves,my fellow citizens. Honour him and love him. Love him truly—do not try to possess him. Trust him as nobly as you trust tomorrow.

"Only the artist in yourselves is more truthful than the night."

1951—from an essay entitled Jottings, published in Wake magazine

equality is what does not exist among equals
most people are perfectly afraid of silence
great men burn bridges before they come to them
the pigpen is mightier than the sword

when Americans stop being themselves they start behaving
each other
false is alike. False teeth
private property began the instant somebody had a mind of
his own
a poet is a penguin—his wings are to swim with
people who live in steel houses should pull down the light-
ning
enter labor,with an itching heart and a palm of gold;leading
(by the nose)humanity,in a unionsuit
a chain is no weaker than its missing link
hatred bounces
sleep is the mother of courage
an intelligent person fights for lost causes,realizing that oth-
ers are merely effects
think twice before you think
knowledge is a polite word for dead but not buried imagina-
tion

Here endeth the fourth lesson—or, speaking precisely, my
fourth lesson; since it's I who (thanks to you) am learning who
I am. Let me now mercifully conclude our egocentric séance by
reading, from that miraculous labour of love which is Francis
James Child's English And Scottish Ballads, one great tragic
and one great comic anonymity: one pitying and one terrible
warning against inhuman unfeeling.

One of the series of "nonlectures" that Cummings gave at Harvard in 1952–53.

INTRODUCTION TO *THE ENORMOUS ROOM* (Modern Library, 1932)

Don't be afraid.

—But I've never seen a picture you painted or read a word you wrote—

So what?

So you're thirty-eight?

Correct.

And have only just finished your second novel?

Socalled.

Entitled ee-eye-em-eye?

Right.

And pronounced?

"A" as in a, "me" as in me; accent on the "me".

Signifying?

Am.

How does Am compare with The Enormous Room?

Favorably.

They're not at all similar, are they?

When The Enormous Room was published, some people wanted a war book; they were disappointed. When Eimi was published, some people wanted Another Enormous Room; they were disappointed.

Doesn't The Enormous Room really concern war?

It actually uses war: to explore an inconceivable vastness which is so unbelievably far away that it appears microscopic.

When you wrote this book, you were looking through war at something very big and very far away?

When this book wrote itself, I was observing a negligible portion of something incredibly more distant than any sun; something more unimaginably huge than the most prodigious of all universes—

Namely?

The individual.

Well! And what about Am?

Some people had decided that The Enormous Room wasn't a just-war book and was a class-war book, when along came Eimi—aha! said some people; here's another dirty dig at capitalism.

And they were disappointed.

Sic.

Do you think these disappointed people really hated capitalism?

I feel these disappointed people unreally hated themselves—

And you really hated Russia.

Russia, I felt, was more deadly than war; when nationalists hate, they hate by merely killing and maiming human beings; when internationalists hate, they hate by categorying and pigeonholing human beings.

So both your novels were what people didn't expect.

Eimi is the individual again; a more complex individual, a more enormous room.

By a—what do you call yourself? painter? poet? playwright? satirist? essayist? novelist?

Artist.

But not a successful artist, in the popular sense?

Don't be silly.

Yet you probably consider your art of vital consequence—

Improbably.

—To the world?

To myself.

What about the world, Mr. Cummings:

I live in so many: which one do you mean?

I mean the everyday humdrum world, which includes me and you and millions upon millions of men and women.

So?

Did it ever occur to you that people in this socalled world of ours are not interested in art?

Da da.

Isn't that too bad!

How?

If people were interested in art, you as an artist would receive wider recognition—

278

Wider?

Of course.

Not deeper.

Deeper?

Love, for example, is deeper than flattery.

Ah—but (now that you mention it) isn't love just a trifle oldfashioned?

I dare say.

And aren't you supposed to be ultramodernistic?

I dare say.

But I dare say you don't dare say precisely why you consider your art of vital consequence—

Thanks to I dare say my art I am able to become myself.

Well well! Doesn't that sound as if people who weren't artists couldn't become themselves?

Does it?

What do you think happens to people who aren't artists? What do you think people who aren't artists become?

I feel they don't become: I feel nothing happens to them; I feel negation becomes of them.

Negation?

You paraphrased it a few moments ago.

How?

"This socalled world of ours."

Labouring under the childish delusion that economic forces don't exist, eh?

I am labouring.

Answer one question: do economic forces exist or do they not?

Do you believe in ghosts?

I said economic forces.

So what?

Well well well! Where ignorance is bliss . . . Listen, Mr. Lowercase Highbrow—

Shoot.

—I'm afraid you've never been hungry.

Don't be afraid.

E. E. CUMMINGS

NEW YORK   1932

WHY DO YOU PAINT?

Why do you paint?
For exactly the same reason I breathe.
That's not an answer.
How long hasn't there been any answer?
As long as I can remember.
And how long have you written?
As long as I can remember.
I mean poetry.
So do I.
Tell me, doesn't your painting interfere with your writing?
Quite the contrary: they love each other dearly.
They're very different.
Very: one is painting and one is writing.
But your poems are rather hard to understand, whereas your
paintings are so easy.
Easy?
Of course—you paint flowers and girls and sunset; things
that everybody understands.
I never met him.
Who?
Everybody.
Did you ever hear of nonrepresentational painting?
I am.
Pardon me?
I am a painter, and painting is nonrepresentational.
Not all painting.
No: housepainting is representational.
And what does a housepainter represent?
Ten dollars an hour.
In other words, you don't want to be serious––
It takes two to be serious.
Well, let's see . . . oh yes, one more question: where will you
live after this war is over?
In China; as usual.
China?
Of course.
Whereabouts in China?
Where a painter is a poet.

Cummings' preface to the catalogue of his 1945 exhibition at the Memorial Art Gallery in Rochester, New York.

NO
THANKS

TO
Farrar & Rinehart
Simon & Schuster
Coward–McCann
Limited Editions
Harcourt, Brace
Random House
Equinox Press
Smith & Haas
Viking Press
Knopf
Dutton
Harper's
Scribner's
Covici-Friede

This dedication acknowledges the fourteen publishers rejecting *No Thanks* (1935), Cummings typically revealing professional as well as esthetic courage.

MEMOIR

The classic example of a really fine book that could not sell was E. E. Cumming's [sic] Enormous Room. But Cumming's book was written in a style that no one who had not read a good deal of "modern" writing could read. That was hard luck for selling purposes.

—Ernest Hemingway, in a letter to Horace Liveright
(March 31, 1925)

Cummings wrote two memoirs—one became popular and beloved, the other did not. In both the prose is often extraordinary. The first, *The Enormous Room* (1922), about his experiences in World War I, was acclaimed by Ernest Hemingway among others. But the initial edition, published by Boni & Liveright in New York, was a bowdlerization allowed by Cummings' father, a Unitarian minister, while Cummings was in Paris. Cummings, outraged, saw to it that a reasonably faithful version was published in England in 1928, one that appeared in the United States in 1934. That edition corrects most of the errors in the first and restores the bilingual writing, incorporating extended passages in French, that make Cummings' memoir a milestone in American experimental literature and incidentally a precursor of recent bilingual books by John Sayles and Raymond Federman, among other contemporaries. It was only in 1978 that an edition authentic in all its details—this one edited by George Firmage—was published. The second memoir, *Eimi* (1933), which my colleague John Rocco writes of below, recalls Cummings' unpleasant trip to Soviet Russia in a style that is at times obscure, at times original and fresh.

—Richard Kostelanetz

*   *   *

Eimi means "I am" in Greek and it represents the great conflict between Cummings' belief in the individual and the deadening machine of the Soviet state. Just as *The Enormous Room* was based upon *Pilgrim's Progress,* Cummings' account of his trip to what he called the Unworld was based upon a work he had been fascinated with since Harvard: Dante's *Inferno* ("Great Dante stands in Florence, looking down / In marble on the centuries"). The portions printed here begin with Comrade K's visit to Lenin's Tomb. As Richard Kennedy has described it, this scene parallels the visit by Dante into the lowest ring of Hell to view Satan. Notice the spiraling downward:

> the
> > Tomb
> > > Crypt
> > > > Shrine
> Grave.

Kennedy also points out that the incredibly inventive and idiosyncratic language of *Eimi*—a new language only comparable to the night world of *Finnegans Wake* and the idiom of Cummings' own radical verse—seems to have its beginnings in the experimental prose of Cummings' letters. Consider that just as Dante's use of the vernacular was revolutionary for the epic poem, Cummings' use of a Cummings vernacular in *Eimi* revolutionizes the travel book and epitomizes his struggle against the forces threatening his Greek title.

—John Rocco

[Paris]
14 mai 1922

I desire that one of two things happen to "The Enormous Room":either

    A)it be immediately supressed,thrown in a shitoir

    B)each and all of the below-noted errors be <u>immediately and completely</u> rectified without loss of time,fear of money,or any-thing-damned-else—

<u>Omissions</u> for which there is no reason and no excuse—

    1)portrait of Jan(not Jean)
    who is nevertheless mentioned,p134

    2)portrait of the Belgian Farmer,who is briefly described (with,I think,some others)in connection with an <u>omitted</u> incident—the Surveillant distributes mail,from a window,to men in the court beneath
    The Farmer is mentioned,p143

    3)portrait of The Young Skipper,who is described along with

    4)his Mate,in(I think)chapter VII of the original MS.
    They are mentioned together,p247
    The Young Skipper is further mentioned pp257,266

N.B.—Not having the MS with me,I cannot tell what other characters have been dropped out;but in the case of these four,-anyone who tries to make sense of the book as it stands can see that their portraits have been omitted.

If the portraits omitted were in any way inferior,there might be some(damned little by Jesus)excuse. They are NOT below,and are—in fact—considerably ABOVE,the average in the mutilated book-as-it-stands.

I do not consider that the omission of certain explanatory matter which should follow the "planton-cries" p79 is good for the book;that matter should be put back in,with whatever else has been dropped out,and put back in Goddamnquick. The appeal of the book is largely documentary;as a document let it appear complete or for Christ's Sweet Sake NOT AT ALL. As a piece of writing,I do not argue—I know how it should be,and if anyone thinks he knows better than I,let him <u>F</u> him-or her-self.

<u>Misprints</u> for which there is no excuse of the smallest variety— occur on,averagely,every other page. *[a list of misprints follows]*
* * *

<u>Translation</u> of the French phrases is,at least half the time,very confusing to the reader—it being very important that he should understand that a certain character <u>is speaking French</u> and <u>not English</u>. I had this carefully regulated,and had translated myself as much as was good for the context,and in the MS THERE IS NONE OF THIS NEEDLESS AMBIGUITY. In addition,the translating is. . . .but I refrain. (P.S. AS IT STANDS the book is not merely an eye-sore but an insult.)

From *The Enormous Room*

That evening,about six o'clock,I heard a man crying as if his heart were broken. I crossed The Enormous Room. Half-lying on his paillasse,his great beard pouring upon his breast,his face lowered,his entire body shuddering with sobs,lay The Wanderer. Several of les hommes were about him,standing in attitudes ranging from semi-amusement to stupid sympathy,listening to the anguish which—as from time to time he lifted his majestic head—poured slowly and brokenly from his lips. I sat down beside him. And he told me "Je l'ai acheté pour six cent francs et je l'ai vendu pour quatre cent cinquante—it was not a horse of this race but of the race"(I could not catch the word) "as long as from here to that post—j'ai pleuré un quart d'heure comme si j'avais une gosse morte—and it is seldom I weep over horses—je dis:Bijou,quittes,au r'oir et bon jour". . .

The vain little dancer interrupted about "réformé horses". . ."Excuses donc—this was no réformé horse,such as goes to the front—these are some horses—pardon,whom you give eat,this,it is colique,that,the other,it's colique—this never—he could go forty kilometres a day . . ."

One of the strongest men I have seen in my life is crying because he has had to sell his favourite horse. No wonder les hommes in general are not interested. Someone said:Be of good cheer,Demestre,your wife and kids are well enough.

"Yes—they are not cold;they have a bed like that"(a high gesture toward the quilt of many colours on which we were sitting,such a quilt as I have not seen since;a feathery deepness soft to the touch as air in Spring)"qui vaut trois fois this of mine—but tu comprends,le matin il ne fait pas chaud"—then he dropped his head,and lifted it again crying

"Et mes outils,I had many—and my garments—where are they put,où—où? Kis! And I had chemises . . . this is poor" (looking at himself as a prince might look at his disguise)— "and like this,that—where?

"Si the voiture is not sold . . . I never will stay here for la durée de la guerre. No—bahsht! To resume,that is why I need . . ."

(more than upright in the priceless bed—the twicestreaming darkness of his beard,his hoarse sweetness of voice—his immense perfect face and deeply softnesses eyes—pouring voice)

"my wife sat over there,she spoke to No one and bothered Nobody—why was my wife taken here and shut up? Had she done anything? There is a wife who fait la putain and turns,to everyone and another,whom I bring another tomorrow . . . but a woman qui n'aime que son mari,qui n'attend que son mari"

(the tone bulged,and the eyes together)

"—Ces cigarettes ne fument pas!" I added an apology,having presented him with the package. "Why do you dépense pour these? They cost fifteen sous,you may spend for them if you like,you understand what I'm saying? But some time when you have nothing"(extraordinarily gently)"what then? Better to save for that day . . . better to buy du tabac and faire yourself;these sont fait de la poussière du tabac."

And there was someone to the right who was saying "Demain,c'est Dimanche alors"—wearily. The King lying upon his huge quilt,sobbing now only a little,heard:

"So—ah—il est tombé un dimanche—ma femme est en nourrice,elle donne la petite à téter"(the gesture charmed)"she said to them she would not eat if they gave her that—ça ne vaut rien du tout—il faut de la viande,tous les jours . . ."he mused. I tried to go.

"Assiedes là"(graciousness of complete gesture. The sheer kingliness of poverty. He creased the indescribably soft couverture for me and I sat and looked into his forehead bounded by the cube of square sliced hair. Blacker than Africa. Than imagination.)

After this evening I felt that possibly I knew a little of The Wanderer, or he of me.

*   *   *

In addition to being called "Syph'lis" he was popularly known as "Chaude Pisse,the Pole". If there is anything particularly terrifying about prisons,or at least imitations of prisons such as

La Ferte,it is possibly the utter obviousness with which(quite unknown to themselves)the prisoners demonstrate willy-nilly certain fundamental psychological laws. The case of Surplice is a very exquisite example:everyone,of course,is afraid of les maladies vénériennes—accordingly all pick an individual(of whose inner life they know and desire to know nothing,whose external appearance satisfies the mind à propos what is foul and disgusting)and, having tacitly agreed upon this individual as a Symbol of all that is evil,proceed to heap insults upon him and enjoy his very natural discomfiture . . . but I shall remember Surplice on his both knees sweeping sacredly together the spilled sawdust from a spittoon-box knocked over by the heel of the omnipotent planton;and smiling as he smiled at la messe when Monsieur le Curé told him that there was always Hell . . .

He told us one day a great and huge story of an important incident in his life,as follows:

"monsieur,réformé moi—oui monsieur—réformé—travaille, beaucoup de monde,maison,très haute,troisième étage,tout le monde,planches,en haut—planches pas bonnes—chan-celle,tout"—(here he began to stagger and rotate before us) "commence à tomber,tombe,tombe,tout,tous,vingt-sept hom-mes-briques-planches-brouettes-tous—dix mètres—zuhzuh-zuhzuhzuhPOOM!—tout le monde blessé,tout le monde tué,pas moi,réformé—oui monsieur"—and he smiled,rubbing his head foolishly. Twenty-seven men,bricks,planks and wheel-barrows. Ten metres. Bricks and planks. Men and wheelbar-rows . . .

Also he told us,one night,in his gentle,crazy,shrugging voice, that once upon a time he played the fiddle with a big woman in Alsace-Lorraine for fifty francs a night;"c'est la misère"—add-ing quietly,I can play well,I can play anything,I can play n'imp-orte quoi.

Which I suppose and guess I scarcely believed—until one afternoon a man brought up a harmonica which he had pur-chased en ville;and the man tried it;and everyone tried it;and it was perhaps the cheapest instrument and the poorest that money can buy,even in the fair country of France;and everyone was disgusted—but,about six o'clock in the evening,a voice came from behind the last experimenter;a timid hasty voice

"monsieur,monsieur,permettez?"

the last experimenter turned and to his amazement saw Chaude Pisse the Pole,whom everyone had(of course)forgotten—

The man tossed the harmonica on the table with a scornful look(a menacingly scornful look)at the object of universal execration;and turned his back. Surplice,trembling from the summit of his filthy and beautiful head to the naked soles of his filthy and beautiful feet,covered the harmonica delicately and surely with one shaking paw;seated himself with a surprisingly deliberate and graceful gesture;closed his eyes,upon whose lashes there were big filthy tears . . .

. . . and suddenly

He put the harmonica softly upon the table. He rose. He went quickly to his paillasse. He neither moved nor spoke nor responded to the calls for more music,to the cries of "Bis!"— "Bien joué!"—"Allez!"—"Vas-y!" He was crying,quietly and carefully,to himself . . . quietly and carefully crying,not wishing to annoy anyone . . . hoping that people could not see that Their Fool had temporarily failed in his part.

*   *   *

—Jean,grasping the pipe and speaking angrily into it,being evidently nettled at the poor connection—"Heh-loh,hello, hello,hello"—surveying the pipe in consternation—"Merde. Ça marche pas"—trying again with a deep frown—"heh-LOH!"—tremendously agitated—"HEHLOH!"—a beatific smile supplanting the frown—"hello Barbu. Est-ce que tu es là? Oui? Bon!"—evincing tremendous pleasure at having succeeded in establishing the connection satisfactorily—"Barbu? Est-ce que tu m'écoutes? Oui? Qu'est-ce que c'est Barbu? Comment? Moi? Qui,MOI? JEAN? jaMAIS! jamais,jaMAIS,Barbu. J'ai jamais dit que vous avez des puces. C'était pas moi,tu sais. JaMAIS,c'était un autre. Peut-être c'était Mexique"—turning his head in Mexique's direction and roaring with laughter— "Hello,HEH-LOH. Barbu? Tu sais,Barbu,j'ai jamais dit ça. Au contraire,Barbu. J'ai dit que vous avez des totos"—another roar of laughter—"Comment? C'est pas vrai? Bon. Alors. Qu'est-ce que vous avez,Barbu? Des poux—OHHHHHHHHH. Je comprends. C'est mieux"—shaking with laughter,then suddenly tremendously serious—"HellohellohellohelloHEHLOH!"—addressing the stovepipe—"C'est une mauvaise machin,ça"—speaking into it with the greatest distinctness—"HEL-L-LOH. Barbu? Liberté,Barbu. Oui. Comment? C'est ça. Liberté pour tou'l'monde. Quand? Après la soupe. Oui. Liberté pour tou' l'monde après la soupe!"—to which jest astonishingly reacted a certain old man known as The West Indian Negro(a stocky credulous creature with whom Jean would have nothing to do,and whose tales of Brooklyn were indeed outclassed by Jean's histoires d'amour)who leaped rheumatically from his paillasse at the word "Liberté" and rushed limpingly hither and thither inquiring Was it true?—to the enormous and excruciating amusement of The Enormous Room in general.

After which Jean,exhausted with laughter,descended from the chair and lay down on his bed to read a letter from Lulu (not knowing a syllable of it). A little later he came rushing up to my bed in the most terrific state of excitement,the whites of his eyes gleaming,his teeth bared,his kinky hair fairly standing on end,and cried:

"You fuck me,me fuck you? Pas bon. You fuck you,me fuck me:—bon. Me fuck me,you fuck you!" and went away capering and shouting with laughter,dancing with great grace and as great agility and with an imaginary partner the entire length of the room.

From *Eimi*

Whom should for dinner magnanimous Harem have invited but
Darksmoothlyestishful(and Her husband
   "more detective-work?" suspicioning I suggest
   "we'll see . . ."
   & what a dinner)
   —they arrive late.
   She looked like the tovarich devil : perhaps he even beat her
up after that party?anyhow she is scared beyond belief of every
one or -thing, she's most commonly and much too- clothed ;
she suffers(And How she suffers)from that ultimate despair of
the spirit which even an impurely an unsimply prodigious
headcold cannot quite symbolize
   nor all Assyrian's gentleness nor Harem's gloating tact nor
comrade Kem-min-kz's comraderie could rout that 1time
sprightly eyeful from its nowish agonies of behavedness. That
formerly eyeful but who(emptily eyelessly)cringes at each
glance(at the glance marital,who imitates 1 now undead fly sub-
subsiding inininto glue)O marriage!
   (. . . her father was killed by the bolsheviks . . .)

facefacefaceface
   hand-
          fin-
             claw
   foot-
      hoof
   (tovarich)
                es to number of numberlessness(un
   -smiling)
   with dirt's dirt dirty dirtier with others' dirt with dirt of
themselves dirtiest waitstand dirtily never smile shufflebudge
dirty pausehalt
   Smilingless.
                Some from nowhere(faces of nothing)others
out of somewhere(somethingshaped hands)these knew igno-

rance(hugest feet and believing)those were friendless(stooping
in their deathskins)all—
numberlessly
—eachotherish
facefacefaceface
facefaceface
faceface
Face
:all(of whom-which move-do-not-move numberlessly)
Toward
the
Tomb
Crypt
Shrine
Grave.
The grave.
Toward the(grave.
All toward the grave)of himself of herself(all toward the
grave of themselves)all toward the grave of Self.
Move(with dirt's dirt dirty)unmoving move un(some from
nowhere)moving move unmoving(eachotherish)
:face
Our-not-their
faceface ;
Our-not-her
, facefaceface
Our-not-his
—toward
Vladimir our life!Ulianov our sweetness!Lenin our hope!
all—
(hand-
fin-
claw
foot-
hoof
tovarich)
es : to number of numberlessness ; un
-smiling

all toward Un- moveunmove , all toward Our haltpause ; all toward All budgeshuffle : all toward Toward standwait. Isn't-ish.

The dark human All warped(the Un-)toward and—faceface-faceface—past Arabian Nights and disappearing . . . number-lessness ; or may possibly there exist an invisible , a final , face ; moveunmovingly which after several forevers will arrive to(hushed)look upon its maker Lenin?

"pahjahlstah"—voice?belonging to comrade K. Said to a most tough cop. Beside shufflebudging end of beginningless-ness , before the Tomb Of Tombs , standunstanding.

(Voice?continues)I , American correspondent . . .

(the toughest cop spun : upon all of and over smallest me staring all 1 awful moment—salutes! And very gently shoves)let the skies snow dolphins—nothing shall confound us now!(into smilelessly the entering beginning of endlessness :

—between these 2 exhausted its : a

bearded , and a merely

unshaven)now who emotionlessly displace themselves. Obe-diently and now we form a dumb me-sandwich. & now which , moves

3 comrades move ; comrade before me(comrade I)comrade behind me . . . un- . . . and move . . . and un- . . . and always(behind comrade behind me)numb-erl-ess-ness

(at either side of the Portal : rigidity. Armed soldier atten-tioning)

—stink ; warm poresbowels , millionary of man-the-unani-mal putrescence. Floods up from dark. Suffocatingly envelopes 3 now(unmovemoving past that attentioning twain each(& whose eyelids moveunmove)other facing rigidities)comrades

as when a man inhabits , for stars and moon , freely him-self(breathing always round air ; living deeply the colour of darkness and utterly enjoying the sound of the great sun ; tast-ing very slowly a proud silence of mountains ; touched by, touching ,what never to be comprehended miracles ; conversing with trees fearlessly and fire and rain and all creatures and each strong faithful thing)as when the man comes to a where tremu-

lous with despair and a when luminous with dissolution—into
all fearfulness comes , out of omnipotence—as when he enters
a city(and solemnly his soul descends : every wish covers its
beauty in tomorrow)so I descended and so I disguised myself ;
so(toward death's deification moving)I did not move
   bearded's cap slumps off. Mine. Beardless's
   . . . now,Stone ; polished(Now)darklyness . . .
   —leftturning:
               Down
(the old skull floating(the old ghost shuffling)just-in-front-
of-me in-stink-and-glimmer &
   from)whom , now : forth creeps , som(ething , timi)dly . . .
a Feeling tenta-
   cle cau , tiously & ,which , softly touchtry-ing fear, ful , ly
how the polished the slippery black , the—is it real?—(da)a-
mazedly & withdraws; diminishes ; wilt
   -ing(rightturn)
               as we enter The Place , I look up : over(all)us
apolished slab reflecting upside(com(moveunmoving)rades)-
down. Now ; a. Pit : here . . . yes—sh!
   under a prismshaped transparency
   lying(tovarich-to-the-waist
   forcelessly shut rightclaw
   leftfin unshut limply
   & a small-not-intense head & a face-without-wrinkles & a
reddish beard).
   (1 appearing quickly uniform shoves our singleness into
2s)yanks bearded to the inside pushes to the outside me . . . &
as un(around the(the prism)pit)movingly comrades the move
   (within a neckhigh wall
   in a groove which surrounds the prism)
   stands , at the prism's neuter pole , a human being(alive ,
silent)with a real rifle :
   —comrades revolve. Wheel we. Now I am somehow(for a
moment)on the inside ; alone—
   growls. Another soldier. Rightturning us. Who leave The
Place(whose walls irregularly are splotched with red frieze)leave

the dumb saccharine porebowel ripeness of stink ... we climb & climbing we
  're out.

Certainly it was not made flesh. And I have seen so many wax-works which were actual (some ludicrous more horrible most both) so many images whose very unaliveness could liberate Is , invent Being(or what equally disdains life and unlife)—I have seen so very many better gods or stranger, many mightier deeper puppets ; everywhere and elsewhere and perhaps in America and(for instance)in Coney Island ...

  now(breathing air,Air,AIR)decide that this how silly unking of Un-,this how trivial idol throned in stink , equals just another little moral lesson. Probably this trivial does not liber-ate , does not invent, because this silly teaches ; because proba-bly this little must not thrill and must not lull and merely must say—

  I Am Mortal. So Are You. Hello
  ... another futile aspect of "materialistic dialectic" ... merely again(again false noun,another fake"reality")the strict immea-surable Verb neglected, the illimitable keen Dream denied

what crispedged flatness does a dexter comrade-hand meet in a sinister comrade-trouserpocket's darkness? 1 ticket(given by Turk as I fled toward another darkness , a different tomb). Blonde and mari , Turkess and Assyrian , are visiting a "musichall" near Something's theatre. I'm due to join them there(comrade Lenin permitting

  and comrade Lenin—hearing the wholly miraculous words "American correspondent"—permits)

the lush with lounging comrades foyer recalls Shaving Hour in a pullman. Somewhere confrère and wholly that bourgeois emerge from a corner near a telephonebooth and

  blandly "our poor sick" Harem said without batting an eye-lash "guest came here with us ; but when we found that the show began at eight-thirty(instead of at seven-thirty as we'd all thought)she went home with her nice husband" "who'll return. And what" Assyrian "to do with one extra seat? . . . I'll try"(flowerbuyer

10 minutelesses)

"he answer nyet." —Comrade(addressing a shrivelled stranger with a huge gorillaface)here

it's too expensive(snortgrunts the gorillaface. Mucho cautiously, nay suspiciously, having surveyed 1 extra ticket)

where do you work?(Turk asks)

(shrugging)I don't

well(that bourgeois more than shrugs)here's the seat—(& 3 comrades invade the pleasantest theatre have yet beheld;leaving 1 comrade dazedly studying a crispedged flatness. Almost immediately enter mari : sits next myself ; agreeable and halitosis. So has the(infinitely wretched and absolutely dragging)show . . . weary "gypsy" dancers , through split skirts waving most unlike legs legs , spiritless "gypsy" songsters and -stresses bellowing semioperatic atrocities—I recognize,with unglee,a pair of god's entertainers . . . next , an educational program of(apparently not for me alone)unmitigated dullness (even the whole audience protests rather feebly after 2nd entr'acte)during which Assyrian disappears to 'phone hole-in-the-forehead and Turkess draws out hal

he's a busy man , hal is. Installing a new(to Russia)automatic railroad signal system. Which is much needed , it seems. For the cheerful Russians decided to replace wornout materials such as cables with other such as cables made by themselves. Result : an intricate ruination of the whole shebang. What do you know—out of every 50 chances to make a mistake , those greedy tovariches took advantage of 4(versus 1 mistake out of 10,000 chances in America). Hal stresses the point that foreigners who are called in to take charge of enterprises find themselves sooner or later helpless before communist doctrine : and they can't ask why such and such workers aren't paid more;and over all "experts" are "bee-essers" who hand out "bee-ess" ad lib , no matter what happens ; and statistics , in this extraordinary country, have become a fetish

"you know how it is here" he sighs "they believe that if a four-cylinder automobile is running on two , it's fifty percent efficient."

"I actually" Turkess "had a communist say to me : we're turning out so many(I can't remember the number)tractors ; what if they don't run? we're turning them out!"

"slightly to change the subject ,why" K asks "did we have the leg stuff first tonight and then the enlightenment business? Was the latter supposed to make us forget the former?"

"my no" cried hal "a few legs don't mean anything to this bunch. Have you seen naked bathing?"

"no"

"you ought to look around" said hal

(who himself has not ; I discover that he's merely heard— from certain of his Russian associates—about places where men and women disport in the alto-, separated only by 2 yards of sand "and a rope"; and a woman will take off everything and will cover her face with a piece of paper and will enjoy a nice quiet sunbath). We glide to marriage

"they've got that all sewed up" blonde's mari affirms "of course , it's not perfect—(nothing is)" he added darkly "but most of the husbands who find themselves divorced feel ,well , relieved . . . I know" dreamily "of a girl who divorced a man and married again ; the second man moved right in—as her husband—and shared her room with the first"

"no news" appearing Turk murmurs. "Poor,poor world"

. . . "why, do you realize"(I'm dangerously leaning on the pedestal of Lenin's huge black bust ,which looks dangerously like Lenin's little pale doll . . . across this corridor dangerously looms comrade Stalin's effigy, the first I've seen—Assyrian and Harem are ½listening to allhetup hal , ½watching 3 uniformed ghosts who simply can't seem to leave our entrancing vicinity)"do you realize"(hal raves)"that there isn't one Russian engineer with more than what you and I would call a highschool education?look : suppose I , an expert , tell them This is the way this has gotta be done . . . know what they do?they go into a conference. Well now,why shouldn't we do it another way ; that's how they talk. It does no good to tell 'em Say listen , I'm not just trying to gratify a personal whim , I'm talking from experience of alotta wise people who taught me—d'y'suppose they'd believe that?huh?HUH?"

the haunting trio approached gradually. Less gradually the
Turk soothed hal into silence . . .

now we're all going
"I've seen nothing native" says K "to compare with your
charming lady"
"no" agrees halitosis gloomily
"who is Polish?"
he nods
"where are all these raving Russian beauties one hears
about?I don't believe they exist"
"sure they do. But they're Asiatic." He shrugged "the Poles
are more refined . . . you know, more European"
"do you think she'll like America?"
"first she's going to Cambridge Ohio to meet" his voice
squirmed "my folks. I tell her" he scowled "in America every-
one will be flirting with her on the street. And" darkly gloomily
shrugging squirming tragically scowling "she'll marry a mil-
lionaire!"

& momentously
"I've come to a truly"
pouring
truly Scotch "momentous conclusion—this land is run by
two
classes :
by exjailbirds and by
shyster
politicians" Assyrian affirms.
("Strange")he said suddenly("I'm only happy in three ways :
when I'm drunk ,when I'm efing ,when I'm working")

* * *

someone
asks something.
—Please , I don't
understand.—"You speak English?"
—"Yes , do you?"—"Yes."—"I
didn't know."—"Now you know."—"Yes"

(a writer. Ecstatic re Russia(and having learned a thing or 3 ,
we'll wait)who arrived by special invitation from New York and
was promptly in Moscow paid 1 "lump" of 2,000 roubles as
royalties for a wellknown opus entitled The Other Side Of The
River or,via the language of unkings , I Am A Jew)

he is ; & a very gentle Jew
(finds out for me that this particular car is the only car with-
out linen. That this particular car is just a Moscow car. That
this particular car's conductor volunteered although this partic-
ular day was his day off)

a very gentle
. . . meanwhile space : and through a ½shut- ½unshut-ness
air ; night ,

we meanwhile pass woods , a fire—smell of!

Why is(angrily)nothing ready?(appearing demands industrial
hero whose badge is almost as big as himself).—Because this
particular . . . (the conductor begins)

we pass this particular village,these particular dark crowds—
a thumping screaming band!

What's going on?(gentle shouts down at 2 boys at 4 eating
the oncreeping softliest untrain eyes)

Soldier(barks bigger briefly)

Our men are going for 3 months(smaller cries)

Want to come to Odessa with me(gentle yells gaily)

"DA"(both)

Why?

"zdyes plokoh"(barks bigger. Smaller nods)

Why?(no answer)why?(shrugging ; wry faces : then)

Nothing to eat(smaller disappearing bawls)

we pass darkness

night
(gentle persuades the particular conductor to look in Hard
and see if he can find an extra blanket. . .particular's Russian
answer is to shut the shutunshutness)

Why is there no light in our compartment?(angrily demands
badger reappearing).—Because this particular car is just . . .

(conductor be-)

    &

"bread?" gentle is offering me something , some bread , some of his tough dark good . . . "chocolate?" am offering gentle something , some chocolate,some of my for export only . . . "together"(he beams:pointing , to bread ; to chocolate)"hahrahshoh!" Good together. Sharing is good. Is better than alone than bread than alone than chocolate than good than alone than than.

He never ate in New York—in Moscow his appetite was simply prodigious

the Writers' Club in Moscow is just as good as Paris(he thinks)or better

have I noticed the "free Russian woman"?no?why she's everywhere! probably she escaped my notice because I was looking for something physically different ; which of course is preposterous : "Nature , always , same"

Leningrad. . .a wonderful place. . .the October hotel with a special for foreigners oldstyle headwaiter a 20 year old with a red scarf girl in charge of the whole Tsar's palace imagine!

"now I go"(sleepsign)

. . .But I must have a light!(badger).—Here is a light(conductor,warily emanating earth's oldest candle , grins).—Thanks! (badger,outreaching greedily).—For all , comrade(the candleman snickers ; mildly grinning , chuckling ; shoving mildly hero aside and sticking ; carefully ; candle into this ; single ; and ; world's ; ancientest ; lantern of just-a-Moscow-particularcar . . .)

BUT—(exploding , hero)

Neecheh-voh(to myself winking , the all-server)

. . .space : &

wigglewoggl

ingl

y the nontrain the untrain the trainless ,

—wogglewiggl

ingl

y the lightless the uncandle the nonlantern
under which sitting ;
under which
under.
I
I ; write
I write wogglewiggl , ingl y

To S. Foster Damon

Guaranty Trust   (but i don't
4placedelaConcorde)
Paris
[1933]

Dear Foster—

re your letter(which just arrived)allow me to congratu-
late eimi! a lucky book!

can report only vaguely on reception-in-general:
apparently one "Nathan" spectatorously called her
"the worse book of the month" before e was ever pub-
lished;other nongentleunmen of ny's pressless sought
gants [sic] ("the funniest book of the month")—fearing
another him?—while curt cowflaps rolled in from ye
sticks inc as per etc . . . Silk Hat Harry(they tell)be-
holding a Hound & a Horn,sprach "of course I don't
mind for myself:but he really shouldn't have made
fun of poor Gene Tunney" so the wellknown thorn
was on trotsky's wing again but

you sound fine not to say hearty—so am I!

Paris amazing. Almost a vacuum where the Americans aren't;
those who are weep concerning $(soon we'll be rid of them
even)hence nothing could suit better

Your humble and obedient servant
who trusts to receive his copy of New Hampshire
alias
Jock duh Frog
Count Sandy d'Essence
Putana Madonna
A.R.Bitz
Herr von der Urinoir
a gentleman with a hat or so
long

Index

INDEX OF POEMS
by Opening Lines and Titles

a gr 130
a he as o 131
a thrown a 118
air, 142
american critic ad 1935 21
Among 97
An(fragrance)Of 109
&(all during the 108
& sun & 125
applaws) 105
ardensteil-henarub-izabeth 126
as 66
as if as 137
as usual i did not find him in the cafes, the more dissolute atmosphere 191
a-t-l-e-t-l-a-v-c-a 151
at the ferocious phenomenon of 5'clock i find myself gently decompos- 201
at the head of this street a gasping organ is waving moth-eaten 197

b 143
(b 165
BALLAD OF AN INTELLECTUAL 30
!blac 174
brIght 85
buncha hardboil guys from duh A.C. fulla 212

chas sing does(who 144
cont)- 86

devil crept in eden wood 48
dim 178
don't get me wrong oblivion 208
dying is fine)but Death 196

e 134
EARLY SUMMER SKETCH 32
emptied.hills.listen. 26
e-r-e-l-l-e-t-u-s-a 150
ev erythinex Cept: 56

f 128
F is for foetus(a 40
(fea 106
first she like a piece of ill-oiled 67
fl 101
floatfloafloflf 164
from the cognoscenti 163

gee i like to think of dead it means nearer because deeper firmer 192
god gloats upon Her stunning flesh. Upon 36
goo-dmore-ning(en 116
go(perpe)go 83
grEEn'sd 102
guilt is the cause of more disauders 3

helves surling out of eakspeasies per(reel)hapsingly 11
her 61
her careful distinct sex whose sharp lips comb 23
(hills chime with thrush) 133
hips lOOset OOping shoulders blonde& pastoral hair,strong, 53
how 47

i 63
I have seen her a stealthily frail 7
i like my body when it is with your 8
i shall imagine life 169
i thank You God for most this amazing 182
i was sitting in mcsorley's   outside it was New York and beauti- 199
i will be 62
if a cheerfulest Elephantangelchild should sit 10
if the 115
if(you are i why certainly 58
in Just- 79
in making Marjorie god hurried 9
insu nli gh t 135
inthe,exquisite; 55
innerly 110
into a truly 70
it)It will it 111
it is at moments after i have dreamed 180
it's jolly 94
it's just like a coffin's 190

k-o-i-k-n-i-s-p-a 155
kumrads die because they're told) 28

l(a 136
life hurl my 84
light cursed falling in a singular block 37
lis 93
logeorge 87
Lord John Unalive(having a fortune of fifteengrand 80
love was—entire excellently steep 68

may i feel said he 46
,mean- 98
mr youse needn't be so spry 4
moan 49
moon over gai 81
mOOn Over tOwns mOOn 77
mortal(s) 41
my deathly body's deadly lady 19
my eyes are fond of the east side 194

n 127
n w 141
NOISE 188
nonsun blob a 168
nouns to nouns 78
now two old ladies sit peacefully knitting 207

o 158
O It's Nice To Get Up In,the slipshod mucous kiss 74
o pr 90
! o(round)moon,how 124
O Thou to whom the musical white spring 16
of evident invisibles 34
o-h-o-t-n-a-f-g-a 152
oil tel duh woil doi sez 20
ondumonde" 91
one 159
out of bigg 45

Perhaps it was Myself sits down in this chair.   There were two chairs in fact 54

r-h-i-p-n-a-s-k-a-n 154
r-k-ch-e-s-v-o 156
r-p-o-p-h-e-s-s-a-g-r 149
r-ü-p-f-e-s-a-g-h-r 153

says ol man no body— 119
serene immediate silliest and whose 5
sh estiffl 88
she being Brand 51
"she had that softness which is falsity" 72
She smiled. She was too full of Bud and siph 13
she,straddling my lap, 6
16 heures 95
skies may be blue;yes 69
SNOW 160
Space being(don't forget to remember)Curved 22
s.ti:rst;hiso,nce;ma:n 129
structure,miraculous challenge,devout am 14
sunset)edges become swiftly 107
swi(92
(swooning)a pillar of youngly 65

ta 100
that famous fatheads find that each 27
that melancholy 121
that which we who're alive in spite of mirrors 12
the bed is not very big 38
the boys i mean are not refined 29
the comedian stands on a corner,the sky is 24
the dirty colours of her kiss have just 205
the dress was a suspicious madder,importing the cruelty of roses 60
the moon is hiding in 71
the(oo)is 161
the poem her belly marched through me as 39
THE RAIN IS A HANDSOME ANIMAL 203
the sky 144, 145
thethe 104
"think of it:not so long ago 210
this(that 89
through the tasteless minute efficient room 59
tw 147
twi- 113
two   brass   buttons   off 148

un(bee)mo 120
up into the silence the green 57
utterly and amusingly i am pash 18

wanta 157
warped this perhapsy 103
when 25
when you went away it was morning 17
whereas by dark really released, the modern 35
wherelings whenlings 171
who(at 132
who is this 123
why did you go 176
will i ever forget that precarious moment? 213

you 146
you asked me to come:it was raining a little, 15
youful 50